ACHIEVING ECONOMY, EFFICIENCY AND EFFECTIVENESS IN THE PUBLIC SECTOR

by Cyril Tomkins
Professor of Accounting and Finance
University of Bath and consultant to
KMG Thomson McLintock

Published by
THE INSTITUTE OF CHARTERED ACCOUNTANTS
OF SCOTLAND
27 QUEEN STREET, EDINBURGH EH2 1LA

FIRST PUBLISHED 1987
THE INSTITUTE OF CHARTERED ACCOUNTANTS OF SCOTLAND
©1987   C R TOMKINS
ISBN 0 9501090 4 5

FOREWORD

This publication is the first of an "Emerging Issues" series which has been initiated by the Research Committee of The Institute of Chartered Accountants of Scotland. The series is addressed to all groups with an interest in accounting information.

At a time of change and of increasing interest in accounting information, the Research Committee believes that this series will meet a need for explanation of issues which are particularly topical. The books in the series will, however, be written in such a way as to be understandable to readers who are not familiar with the extensive academic theoretical literature. Although primarily intended for accountants, bankers, civil servants, directors and managers, and investors and their advisors, they will also be useful for students.

This particular book by Professor Cyril Tomkins, which sets the recent developments in public sector auditing and reviews within the context of both management and accountability within the public sector, is both topical and thought-provoking. As such it should be required reading for public sector managers and politicians.

The Committee commends this book for study and discussion in the interests of better understanding; the opinions expressed by the author are, of course, his own.

The Institute of Chartered
Accountants of Scotland

Jack Shaw
Convener, Research Committee

ABOUT THE AUTHOR

Cyril Tomkins is Professor of Accounting and Finance in the School of Management at the University of Bath. He has served as Head of the School of Management for six of his ten years at the University and previously held academic posts at several universities including Strathclyde. He is a member of both The Chartered Institute of Public Finance and Accountancy and The Chartered Association of Certified Accountants and retained as consultant to KMG Thomson McLintock on public sector matters. Professor Tomkins has conducted or supervised many research projects in both the public and private sectors including research funded by a Royal Commission, The Social Sciences Research Council (now the ESRC), the CBI, the Equipment Leasing Association, the British Council and Overseas Development Administration as well as by Government Departments and specific local and health authorities. He currently maintains research and consultancy interests in both the public and private sectors with the main focus being on financial management and control in large organisations irrespective of the sector or part of the world in which they are located. As either sole or joint author he has published several previous books covering topics as diverse as the construction of social accounts for Wales, a study of the leasing industry, financial planning in divisionalised companies and issues in public sector accounting. He has also authored sixty articles - mainly in refereed academic, but partly in the professional, journals. He has lectured on management development programmes or to academic conferences in many countries including the USA, most European countries (particularly on behalf of Management Centre Europe), Scandinavia, the Middle East, Far East and Australia.

PREFACE

Early in January 1986 I received an unexpected letter from Jack Shaw asking me to consider writing a book for The Institute of Chartered Accountants of Scotland on managing economy, efficiency and effectiveness in the public sector. I presumed that the emphasis on management, rather than value for money auditing, was deliberate, but I also presumed that accountants were mainly interested in value-for-money audit and management consultancy with regard to the public sector. It was through thinking around these two points that the purpose of this book was developed. That is, I would attempt to set the recent developments in public sector auditing and reviews within the context of both management and accountability within the public sector.

As someone who is primarily an accountant specialising in financial control issues, I hesitated before proceeding along this path. The issues of general management and social accountability go far beyond accounting and financial control and there are many experts in these wider fields. There has, however, been much recent criticism of the current state of accounting literature, even amongst academic accountants, and one major reason for this has been that accountants have traditionally tended to see their discipline as a largely technical process in isolation from the context in which it operates and with little recognition of other disciplines concerned with management of organisations.

Practitioners, forced to operate in the real world, where managers with different functional interests cannot avoid some interaction, do have to modify the practices that we see described in textbooks, but it is time that accounting literature took greater account of that reality. In so doing it might facilitate a better understanding of how the expertise of the different disciplines can be welded together to provide effective management and accountability.

i

Until more academic accountants are prepared to take a risk with their reputations by moving outside the narrower confines of their own technical specialism, our accounting thought will continue to exhibit the drawbacks of retaining a limited functional perspective. Members of other disciplines and professions are unlikely to do this for us when they are in competition with us and would just as soon see us wither or lose separate identity within some broader grouping of information providers. Of course, there are many complex technical problems still to be solved within a more narrowly defined field of accounting and auditing, but unless the role and context of accounting is better understood, accountants and accounting academics may be spending valuable resources providing solutions to problems which do not need to be addressed to improve our human condition or which, though logically appearing to be desirable, stand no chance of implementation.

I did not, therefore, hesitate long in deciding to address first some broader aspects of management and accountability although in doing so I was forced to place considerable reliance on ideas developed by others in neighbouring disciplines. The pursuit of this goal took me into economics, social science evaluation, politics (to a limited extent) and finally into organisation theory. I was repeatedly forced to recognise my own limitations in terms of knowledge of those disciplines. On the other hand I have now had twenty-five years' experience both working in and observing public sector organisations. Consequently, one is not a complete neophyte on such questions, nor beyond looking at some literature from these neighbouring fields in critical fashion.

It would be ridiculous, however, in a small book, to attempt to provide a fully comprehensive discussion of 'good management practices'. What is provided are some fundamental principles and ideas which are sufficient to act as a backcloth against which to consider the role of auditing and consultancy by accounting firms within the general management and accountability of public sector organisations. Even so, some aspects of management described in this book place a different emphasis on what is needed for 'good management' in comparison with more traditional views of managerial control. It is hoped, therefore, to provoke debate and thought about general management practice as well as the role of auditing and consulting. In fact, even if the aggregate view of the profession or members of other disciplines proves to be against those offered in this book, I shall be content if it does create debate and thought, for rarely after such a process is knowledge or opinion left completely unchanged. It is in this spirit in which this book is offered and I thank Jack Shaw for encouraging me to embark on the exercise and Professors David Flint and Andrew McCosh, the Institute representatives and advisers, for allowing me considerable freedom to write what I wished. In so doing, however, I would not want them to be saddled with supporting all the views I put forward; the sole responsibility for them is mine.

In this spirit also I will be very pleased to receive any comments, whether highly critical or otherwise, should any reader feel inclined to send some to me. In particular I would appreciate comments from practitioners for there is insufficient interaction between academia and practising accountants and managers. Academic theories are bound to remain weak over-generalised descriptions and explanations of practice as long as that state continues.

Cyril Tomkins
School of Management
University of Bath

Christmas 1986

CONTENTS

1 WHERE DOES THE PRIVATE SECTOR END AND THE PUBLIC SECTOR BEGIN?

A text devoted to the management of the public sector suggests that there is a clear distinction between that sector and the private sector. This chapter questions whether such clarity usually exists in public debates and offers proposals for how it can be achieved. It seems critical, before discussing management in the public sector, that one both forms a view as to where the dividing line between the public and private sector should come and also locates that discussion within the context of the broader economic and political debate relating to the control of public sector expenditure. Moreover, there is little point writing about the problems of managing the public sector, if there is a clear answer in privatising it. The clarification of these issues is the purpose of this first chapter.

Since the election of the Conservative Government in 1979, there has been a considerable examination of public sector expenditure. This seems to have been fuelled by two main motivating factors. First, there was a new emphasis on restricting the Public Sector Borrowing Requirement in order to improve management over the whole economy (the macro-economic perspective) and, second, there was the stronger assertion that increased exposure of public sector activities to market forces was more capable of stimulating improvements in efficiency (the micro-economic perspective). This text focuses on the micro-economic aspects, but it is interesting to address the macro-economic perspective, albeit briefly, to examine whether arguments there are likely to override or support any arguments about the location of the boundary between the two sectors.

WHERE DOES THE PRIVATE SECTOR END AND THE PUBLIC SECTOR BEGIN?

Macro-economic Efficiency

The popular argument relating to the control of public expenditure, often presented by industrialists and politicians in the press and on television, goes something like this. Industry creates wealth, the public sector cannot consume it unless it is created, hence, if too much is spent on public sector services, there will be fewer resources devoted to the private sector to increase wealth either by investment for future growth or yielding foreign earnings. This general argument is often referred to as the public sector 'crowding out' the private sector and there are two levels of 'crowding out' which need separate consideration: direct 'crowding out' and indirect 'crowding out'.

Direct 'crowding out' refers simply to the use of labour or capital by the public sector which could have been used by the private sector. This implies first that all current labour and capital resources are fixed in supply and fully utilised. There is something in the argument that neither of these situations strictly apply, especially with the current level of unemployment, although this can be partly countered by the argument that labour is not fully mobile and so the effective supply is more fully utilised than might appear to be the case. Leaving such arguments aside, however, the key factor in determining future increases in wealth is the relationship between that amount of current wealth consumed and that re-invested and not expenditure classified by public or private sector per se. Not all public expenditure is current consumption; capital investment takes place in the public sector and, moreover, elements of its current expenditure provides the necessary 'infrastructure' of health, education, roads, etc, which facilitates the operation of the private sector. In addition, not all private sector expenditure is necessarily channelled into areas which are most likely to generate future growth of foreign earnings. So even on the general direct 'crowding out' argument, there is a need for careful consideration of concepts. It is quite possible that a Government may want to transfer resources from the public to the private sector in order to promote more growth, but the justification should rest on the choice between specific types of expenditure and their likely economic and social effects and not the sector to which they are assigned.

The main indirect 'crowding out' arguments are threefold. First, it is argued that increases in public expenditure increase taxation which reduces personal motivation and corporate returns on investment and thereby reduces effort and investment. There may be some justification in this, but the full effect depends, once more, upon what the Government spends the taxes. The key question is: does one believe that the Government or the market mechanism is best able to make decisions to promote the required balance of consumption and growth? The argument should focus directly on that and not treat increased taxation as inherently bad.

The second indirect argument states that the increase in public expenditure will increase public debt which increases interest rates and decreases investment. Again there is an element of truth in the argument, but care is also needed once more. The increase in expenditure may be balanced by increased taxation and then no increase in public sector debt occurs and the arguments of the previous paragraph come into play. Moreover, even if the public sector debt does increase, it may be in respect of investment in nationalised industries or other 'infrastructure investment' which, as argued before, may be just as desirable as investment in the private sector. In fact most European countries exclude debt in respect of 'nationalised industries' from their PSBR figures.

WHERE DOES THE PRIVATE SECTOR END AND THE PUBLIC SECTOR BEGIN?

The third dimension of indirect 'crowding out' argues that increased public expenditure is often financed through increasing the money supply which fuels inflation. Hence, the PSBR must be constrained. Again there is merit in the argument, but it should also be noted that if the increased expenditure is not financed from bank sources the money supply does not increase. Some economists are also far from convinced about the effect of a change in the money supply on inflation, but that is another matter.

So what may one conclude from this very brief review of macro-economic arguments? All the arguments have some element of validity; an excessive increase in public expenditure will 'crowd out' the private sector both directly and quite possibly indirectly, but there is no *a priori* macro-economic reason why some activities should be in the private sector and some in the public sector. Furthermore, the level of expenditure on the public sector at any time should reflect the values attached by individuals and national agencies to alternative consumption streams in real terms. Macro-economics, in effect, tries to identify the consumption streams which result from different distributions of expenditure. It should not choose between the consumption streams. If one seeks to establish a boundary between the private and public sectors through economic reasoning, one must, therefore, turn to micro-economic arguments related to the efficiency of the market mechanism.

Micro-economic Efficiency

At the micro-economic level there are still two types of efficiency to be distinguished (see Tomlinson (1986) for a more extended argument than that given here). First, there is market, or allocative, efficiency which concerns the distribution of products produced, ie how many cars and cakes and who should

---

get them? In contrast, there is internal, or managerial,
efficiency, ie given that we want cakes, what is the cheapest
way of producing them?

Micro-economic theory concentrates mainly on allocative
efficiency. Using assumptions of perfect markets and an
appropriate distribution of purchasing power, it is possible to
demonstrate that one gets 'the most efficient' production and
allocation of goods and services. Here there is a powerful
argument for more activities being located in the private, rather
than the public, sector. Unfortunately, life is not so easy as
that because, for a variety of reasons, real world markets are not
perfect and wealth is not distributed in a totally equitable way.
This is not intended to be a political argument; all governments
intervene in the market to some extent to ensure those without
the means to pay for certain 'essential' goods have some support.
Moreover, perfect product markets are not enough. There must
also be perfect resource markets if one is to obtain the general
market clearing equilibrium - hence the argument to allow wages
to fluctuate downwards now.

Irrespective of whether or not one can rely on the degree of
competition which exists in markets substantially to increase
allocative efficiency in comparison to that achievable if the
activities in question were located in the public sector, the issue
of whether private sector status is more likely to induce
managerial efficiency still has to be addressed. The empirical
evidence on managerial efficiency is sparse and, especially as
regards the UK, difficult to interpret as it is difficult to compare
like with like in the two different sectors. To add to the
difficulty, such evidence that does exist is confusing. Pryke
(1971 and 1981) studied nationalised industries for the period
1958 - 1968 and concluded that they were more productive than
they would be in the private sector. He then studied the period

1968 - 1978 and came to the opposite conclusion. It was more
important, he stated, for economists to consider the effect of
monopoly status on efficiency, not the sector in which the
organisation was located. A later study, Pryke (1982), did
attempt to compare like with like (ferries, showrooms, air
transporters) and concluded that the private sector was more
efficient, but other studies (see Millward, 1982 and Millward and
Parker, 1983) conducted other like-with-like investigations in the
USA, Australia, etc and concluded that there were no grounds for
believing that managerial efficiency is less in public firms. These
studies do not, of course, cover the recent privatisations where
general observation does seem to indicate some improvement in
performance in industries previously nationalised, but it is too
soon to tell whether that will be sustained or is due to initial
euphoria. Also a very recent study by The London Business
School (see Chapter 2) does indicate large savings from
contracting out refuse collection, but one can hardly generalise
from this to all the public sector.

With the empirical evidence so inconclusive, what theoretical
arguments exist in favour of privatisation. There are several
main ones: that product market competition will induce
managerial efficiency in order to allow the organisation to
survive, that the threat of takeover on The Stock Exchange will
induce managerial efficiency and, finally, that the simple freedom
from bureaucratic public sector (or government) control promotes
initiative and enthusiasm to improve one's position.

The product market competition argument has to be severely
qualified where there are significant economies of scale. There
is then a conflict between the need to reduce the number of
firms in a market in order to lower average product costs and
the need to increase the number of firms to stimulate more
competition and, thereby, lower costs. Recent developments in

---

economics suggest how that conflict may be resolved (see Bailey
and Baumol, 1984 and Bailey, 1986). This newer theory is called
'Contestable Market Theory'. Its argument runs that it is not
product competition which is vital, but competition for a market.
Hence, it follows that there may be enough competitive forces
upon a monopolist provided that there are predators around
watching for opportunities to enter the market if they feel the
monopolist is not operating as efficiently as it might. This
argument in turn rests on there being sufficient freedom of entry
into the market. Government policy should therefore be aimed at
eliminating barriers to entry and not destroying economies of
scale through breaking up large organisations. This argument has
not seen much effect yet in the UK, but it has much to
recommend it. As always, however, problems will exist in some
situations. If, for example, entry requires a large infrastructure
expenditure this may prove to be a severe barrier to entry. To
take an extreme case, it is difficult to see a new entrant into
the rail transportation industry laying down a rail network.
Nevertheless, the Government might take over the infrastructure
and then allow freedom of entry to compete on the
transportation act itself. It is interesting that a market
economics view of inducing efficiency in this situation might lead
to specific new public sector responsibilities rather than
'privatising everything'.

Even if private sector firms are efficient low cost producers in a
short-run sense, this does not mean that they are efficient in
terms of long-run survival. Government sector intervention may
well be needed then. A common complaint of some British
industrialists is that their rivals abroad get more strategic
support from their governments.

Also, the fact that organisations are in the public sector does
not necessarily mean an absence of competition. Universities, for

7

example, compete with each other for students and, of course,
the current Conservative Government has discussed various ideas
for introducing more competition into all levels of education and
other public services.   So one sees, once more, no clear cut
picture.   There is no argument based on market competition
which puts beyond all doubt that either the private sector or the
public sector must be more managerially efficient than the other,
although it does seem that more competition in either sector
provides a beneficial stimulus.

Moving to the next argument, The Stock Exchange is supposed to
be highly efficient as a mechanism for pricing securities.   But
the efficient pricing of a company with an existing degree of
efficiency is not the same as stimulating increased managerial
efficiency itself - that depends upon the stimuli managers feel
about the need to improve and these stimuli may not necessarily
be created by the process of buying and selling shares on The
Stock Exchange.

Attempts to collect evidence on whether profitability improves
after takeovers, for example, has generally resulted in the
conclusion that shareholders do not benefit after takeovers,
although managers often do in terms of increased scale of
business, etc (see, for example, Singh, 1975, or Goddard, 1986).
In addition, often legislation prevents the takeover of privatised
organisations.   The Trustee Savings Bank (not even in the public
sector) legislation prohibited anyone from holding more than 5%
of the ordinary shares in the first five years of operation and
after five years no-one can hold more than 15%.   Shareholders
can change the rule, but they need a 75% majority.   The offer
for sale of British Gas included similar restrictions. Consequently
the stock market threat argument cannot be relied upon to
stimulate significant increases in managerial efficiency in all
situations, although obviously, there will be some effect due to

the increased public scrutiny associated with quoted status.

This brings us to the last argument relating to managerial efficiency, namely that it is stimulated by increased freedom of action. In the public sector, British Coal cannot, for example, diversify into other businesses. In the private sector, in contrast, new opportunities for which existing skills are suitable can be pursued to create an entity which changes its activities through time to match market demand. Moreover, private companies have more freedom to plan ahead in accordance with the requirements of their industry and not be subject to <u>direct</u> intervention to meet short-term macro-economic needs such as the reduction of the PSBR.

There is also more to the argument than that. The author believes that he does see a new entrepreneurial attitude in the newly privatised (or threatened to be privatised) organisations. It may well be that the public sector lost the culture to innovate and that it is easier and quicker to change that culture by a sharp shock like privatisation than through working upon the organisation remaining in the public sector. If so, it is hard to justify by economic analysis as yet, but just one illustration is offered of what can happen on privatisation in response to new freedom to diversify and act entrepreneurially. The reader is referred to the Nippon Telegraph and Telephone Company, the domestic telephone corporation of Japan. After only one year of gaining private status (although unlike British Telecom the shares are being sold off in tranches), the new company has introduced a considerable number of developments. It has increased private telephone lines and substantially increased mobile telephone services, the use of pre-paid magnetic cards for use in public phone boxes, facsimile services, video-tex subscribers and various other services. In addition, NTT has introduced CAPTAIN, which allows subscribers with display terminals to obtain a range of

---

information similar to PRESTEL, but which also provides a library
of software for handling a range of complex calculations.

ANSER, a system whereby large companies can respond to
customers' calls for information and introduced in 1981, is being
extended and is now available for use unmodified by 39 different
types of computers. Considerable work is also going into the
development of the 'Intelligent Building Concept' where all
aspects of building management (fire prevention, security, data
processing, etc) become part of a comprehensive communications
network. The net result of these activities was a 57% increase
over projected income for the first year of privatised operation.
Clearly this corporation is in an area, telecommunications, which
will see dramatic innovation over the next decade and so,
perhaps, one should not be too surprised to see a Japanese
company in this area being so growth conscious. But, even in
Japan, it seems, it was thought necessary to remove such an
organisation from the political and bureaucratic constraints of
public sector status. With this new found freedom and the threat
of competition, the new company is moving very fast to take up
the opportunities it sees before others do. Of course, there may
be something in the Japanese private sector culture which is not
present in the British private sector, in which case the
private/public sector debate may need to be resolved in a
different way in different social/business environments, but let us
hope that the same culture shock occurs in our own British
Telecom, British Gas, etc.

Of course, there may be other ways of 'shocking the system'
such as, possibly, removal of tenure in universities. Hence, if
this psychological argument holds up at all, it is the shock which
is important, not necessarily the move of an organisation across
the divide into the private sector. Nevertheless, it seems that
where the need for social control over operations is not

dominant, the 'culture shift' is more easily and demonstrably achieved by exposure to the private sector. At least then, it is more difficult for the government bureaucracy to re-intervene at a later date.

Conclusions on the Private Sector/Public Sector Boundary

The series of arguments above all point in one direction: there is no clear cut economic logic which states that private sector organisations must be more efficient. On the other hand, the debate surrounding these issues does suggest the need for the development of increased competitive pressures even within the public sector. Ownership, per se, is not the key issue. The important matter is to examine each type of activity and consider exactly what form and extent of social control is needed. It seems that the basic micro-economics arguments relating to free market operation do have considerable merit and the key question is when and how much they have to be qualified. This suggests that one should try to maximise the degree of movement towards the market ideal, but recognise that different sorts of economic activity need degrees of social control. This leads to the deduction of not a simple private-public sector dichotomy, but of a range of organisational forms with completely private and completely public forms of operation being each end of the range. Indeed, since 1979, we have seen a considerable development of this notion, rather than a removal of elements of the public sector to a completely competitive private sector (see Wright, 1986 for a more detailed review).

A full 'continuum' of organisational forms might look like the listing given below, ranging from fully private at the top, to fully public at the bottom:

WHERE DOES THE PRIVATE SECTOR END AND THE PUBLIC SECTOR BEGIN?

A	-	FULLY PRIVATE
B	-	PRIVATE WITH PART STATE OWNERSHIP
C	-	JOINT PRIVATE/PUBLIC VENTURES
D	-	PRIVATE REGULATED
E	-	PUBLIC INFRASTRUCTURE/PRIVATE OPERATING
F	-	CONTRACTED OUT
G	-	PUBLIC: WITH 'MANAGED COMPETITION'
H	-	PUBLIC: WITHOUT COMPETITION

The policy implication might be to place as many organisations as possible in the highest, next highest, etc classification, ie to provide as much freedom as possible. Criteria would be needed, however, to set the limit to the upward movement of any activity through the classifications. For example, where there are no major social issues at stake, no specific needs to be protected and ability to pay is a fair choice mechanism, there should be no limit to prevent such activities being allocated to class A. Class B, in contrast, would be appropriate where there is potential for a social issue to arise and where the need to influence may be unlikely but, if needed, would have to be imposed quickly. Joint ventures might be relevant where there is a need to develop parts of the private sector (eg small businesses or inner city redevelopments), where there are considerable risks involved (eg the ECGD arrangements), or where new skills can be developed best in co-operation. Category D is essentially the classification of British Telecom and British Gas where there will probably be the need for control by organisations like OFTEL. Class E might be used to facilitate a wider adoption of the 'contestable market theory'. Contracted out forms of organisation seem relevant where there is a need to keep a close on-going control over the quality of service and, because well structured activities like catering, road cleansing, building maintenance and refuse collection are more easily monitored, we are more likely to see contracting-out in such areas. This has, in fact, been borne out by practice. The last two categories relate to services both controlled and produced by public sector organisations, but there may well be scope for a lot more to go into category G than in H. It might, for example, seem that Law and Order must go into Class H and certainly this seems self-evident with the criminal justice system. Parts of the provision of law and order may, nevertheless, be moved into Class G or even higher. The protection of property and various civilian aspects of police operation might be contracted out. There is also probably scope for placing much of education, health or other public services into Class G, although to do so might need a very careful analysis of the appropriate competitive devices in order to avoid undesirable effects on service provision.

Clearly, the question of where the boundary between the public sector and private sector should come is a complex question. One has to recognise that political slogans are, often inevitably, simplifications of the arguments analysed in developing them. Yet, the current tendency to view the private/public sector as good/bad according to one's political view needs to be checked and explored more carefully. It appears highly likely that the recent trends to explore 'hybrid' or 'intermediate' forms of private/public control must continue over the long run. The focus should be on the appropriate form of management and control for each activity, rather than ideological support for its location in either the private or public sector.

The remaining question for this chapter is what implication this all has for a text on the management of economy, efficiency and effectiveness in the public sector. The main implication is that one should beware universalities. The ideal form of the text would examine each type of activity in its current context before trying to propose managerial solutions - even then such broad

contingencies might be misleading. Within each class there may
well be factors leading to the need for differentiation in
management practices. That route is not, however, available for
this type of text. There is a severe limit on space and the
intention is to raise and clarify issues not resolve them, even if
directions in which solutions might lie are suggested. Also one
probably needs more time to elapse before the recent shifts of
public organisations, 'through the classes' specified, settle down
and become stable enough for more permanent conclusions to be
drawn. The remaining structure of the text will, therefore,
follow rather a review of developments since 1979 and explore
some key issues which arise from that review with the major
focus on activities in Classes G and H which will be the hard
core of the public sector.

2 IMPROVING EFFICIENCY AND EFFECTIVENESS IN THE PUBLIC SECTOR: THE UK EXPERIENCE, 1979 - 1986[1]

The starting point to this chapter will not be the UK, but the USA, and the position of planning and control in the US public sector about twenty years ago. At that time there was a concern that the traditional approach to resource allocation in the public sector was defective. Budgets were added to in incremental fashion without, it seemed, any clear overall strategy or goals. Indeed it was often not at all clear what activities were being conducted within various budgetary headings - beyond, that is, some very general descriptions and classifications of expenditure. Also, at that time, there was a thrust within the private sector to develop more comprehensive corporate planning approaches so that overall organisation strategy was formulated in clear goals which then became reflected in organisation structure and plans. The goals and plans were themselves to be formulated by a process of ranking a wide number of options available. This form of rational planning logic led to the attempt to apply a Planning, Programming, Budgetary System (PPBS) in first the United States Government and then the idea spread to various countries throughout the world. Social goals were to be formulated and plans and budgets drawn up to coincide with them even if this meant cutting right across existing departmental boundaries.

In the event PPBS applications tended to be developed within main departments rather than right across the whole government

---

[1]   This chapter is based extensively on a review of developments in the UK presented by the author of this book as a talk to an international conference on Productivity, hosted by the American College in Athens, September 1986.

sector, but the basic rationale was the same. In general these PPBS experiments failed. There is a very extensive literature on this question, but those wanting summaries might refer to Van Gunsteren (1976) or Tomkins (1980). Essentially, it seemed that these systems failed for three reasons.

First, the tight, logical, top-down, planning rationality did not take into account the political reality. Social programmes tend to involve time horizons longer than political horizons, but, perhaps more importantly, established government departments and different parts of the public sector are not without power to fight for control over activities which have traditionally been assumed to be theirs. What is logical and rational in a planning sense is not, therefore, necessarily seen as logical and rational within a political view of reality.

Second, the notion of identifying and then ranking a large range of options for achieving goals implied a level of knowledge not easily attainable. Critics of PPBS argued that there were cognitive limits to the degree of analysis that could be undertaken by any person or organisation and a full implementation of PPBS ideas demanded more rational analysis than was feasible.

Third, the planning rationality was said to ignore the processes by which large organisations function. Decision-making, it was said, is not conducted in a neat rational hierarchical manner, but the subject of negotiation and interaction across many interested parties. There is, in other words, the problem of internal organisational 'politics' as well as party and inter-departmental politics to take into account (see Rosenberg and Tomkins, 1983, Colville, 1985 and Williams, 1986, for a range of studies conducted at the University of Bath into such issues. These are considered in a little more depth in Chapter 5).

While the idea of a total goal orientated, integrated planning and budgetary control system was attractive intellectually, it did not, in general, work. The philosophy behind it was good, but the practical difficulties too great - except, perhaps, in very small countries with few ministries or departments with long historical traditions and where democratic notions of government were not well developed. The idea of government programmes still, of course, persists, but the full implementation of the PPBS ideas does not. Nevertheless, the experiment did emphasise the need for some form of better control over efficiency and effectiveness of public spending and a greater degree of rational analysis within that process, but the totally comprehensive 'rationalistic'[2] ideas of PPBS were left aside.

With the failure of PPBS, another budgetary approach developed in the United States called Zero Based Budgeting. The basic idea

---

[2]   The word 'rationalistic' is used here and later in the book to refer to the form of rational planning which attempts to design comprehensive and totally integrated systems based upon prior specification of high level objectives and a subsequent rigorous deduction of sub-goals and activities from those objectives. It refers to an extreme form of rationality in planning and control almost never met anywhere in practice, but its use does not indicate that all forms of rational analysis must be dismissed. This very important point is taken up in some depth in Chapter 5.

17

behind this was again to impose a greater degree of rational choice in achieving effectiveness in the public sector. Again coming to the public sector after initial development in the private sector, this system took a 'bottom up' approach. Within each of the lowest sub-units of the public sector, all activities were to be arranged into distinctly separate costed packages and ranked in order of priority. These ranked lists were then transmitted up through the organisation, with each successive level adjusting the ranked list as thought appropriate until one arrived at a ranked list for the whole Government department. That was the idea; as a complete system it also failed for the same reasons as did PPBS. The intention was good. There was a need to challenge all existing expenditure to see whether it was still needed, but the system again failed through trying to be too comprehensive and too rational.

This is not to say that ZBB has had no success at all. It emphasised the need to re-examine the base expenditure in budgets and where confined to small areas of activity, and applied at intervals rather than every year, it may well be a valuable tool in the control of public sector effectiveness. But it is the idea which is valuable, and the attitude it can create amongst public sector civil servants and officers, rather than the detailed budgetary processes advocated by ZBB supporters.

The UK Experience, 1979 - 1986[3]

To their credit UK Governments never tried to apply PPBS nor ZBB in any serious fashion. New forms of planning and review were developed in the 1970s, but these were very much based upon existing departmental structures (see Wildavsky, 1975). The considerable publicity given to PPBS and ZBB did, however, heighten public awareness of the need to get a grip on the public purse. Then came the oil crises of 1974 and 1979 and the pressure to control public spending intensified.

Having been elected in 1979, Mrs Thatcher also had a natural inclination to turn to the private sector for guidance on how to improve public sector performance. With the earlier lessons of failures abroad in PPBS and ZBB there was, however, caution not to seek a new totally comprehensive planning system even though they had been based on ideas emanating from the private sector. The UK Conservative Government adopted essentially a two-pronged approach. First, it believed in the use of market forces to induce efficiency and so it set about returning as much of the public sector as it could to the private sector - the Privatisation Programme was born. Second, where complete privatisation was inappropriate, a range of approaches have been taken to improve the efficiency (or productivity) of public service delivery. A brief outline of steps taken in each main area of the UK public will now be given. This will provide insights into where further

---

3   Peat Marwick Mitchell (1984 and 1986) and papers in Mayston and Terry (1986) provided summaries of events during this period and were useful in developing a framework for this chapter.

thinking and consultancy in public sector management might focus.

1.   Central Government

In 1980, Lord Rayner, of Marks and Spencer, was appointed as Mrs Thatcher's Special Adviser on Efficiency.   He established what came to be known as 'the Rayner scrutinies', and these had one marked advantage over traditional attempts which had tried to improve efficiency through O&M and Operations Research departments in that it was clear that there was direct Prime Ministerial backing and interest.   It was said that Rayner merely did what was tried before but 'without clout'.   An extensive discussion of the Rayner scrutinies is provided in Metcalfe and Richards (1984).   Only brief details can be provided in this general review.

First, the Rayner scrutinies did not attempt to impose a unified technical approach.   Each Government department was asked to propose a significant area of investigation and propose a person (usually a high-flying officer still in his 30s) with clear responsibility to develop proposals for improving efficiency in that area within a fairly short time span of 90 days.   Departments were urged to propose problems which could actually be managed and make practical and specific proposals for savings.   They were not encouraged to develop grand overall schemes of total efficiency.

Using this basis of encouraging departments to conduct their own reviews, the Efficiency Unit was headed by Lord Rayner (on an unpaid, part-time basis) and it needed only six full-time Civil Servants to run it. It was, therefore, a very low cost method of looking for increased efficiency.

Lord Rayner left this post in 1983, but the Unit has continued under Sir Robin Ibbs. While the 'scrutinies' remain the central feature of the work, the emphasis has now shifted from ad hoc efficiency studies, with associated cost-cutting connotations, towards an integration of these scrutinies with a more complete system of value for money reviews where priorities for investigations and performance targets are set and achievement monitored. This has tended to emphasise how difficult it is for Government departments to do that and how much they need to devote attention to performance measurement and evaluation.

The success of the approach depended very much upon the direct link with the Prime Minister and this led to the identification of possible savings of £600 million. The identification of potential savings is not, however, the same as the achievement of savings. In a report by the National Audit Office (1986), it was stated that less than half the potential savings are now expected to be achieved. The National Audit Office examined scrutiny reports which indicated total possible savings of £216 million, but only £99 million worth of these recommendations were accepted. This shortfall was, according to the Audit Office, due to a number of factors. Various scrutiny reports were not given prompt attention (some 1980 reports are still waiting for their recommendations to be given a clear decision one way or the other). Those taken up were often not given an appropriately short action plan to ensure implementation. Not surprisingly, some recommendations were rejected. In other cases there is the need for new legislation or new computer systems which take time. Also some forecasted savings were over-ambitious.

The results of the scrutiny programme are, therefore, mixed. Nevertheless it seems clear that the scrutiny approach is one useful way of examining the scope for savings, even if it is clear that the implementation stage of the process needs more careful planning than it appears to have received to date in the UK.

Also the approach offers a fairly inexpensive way of a continued search for efficiency. Events occur and activities change through time and so there is no reason why there are not always going to be possibilities for fresh ideas to improve efficiency. How successful the Ibbs era of scrutinies will be remains to be seen. While one can sympathise with the need for giving more top level direction to give focus to the scrutinies, if this is pushed too far he will run the risk of going the PPBS/ZBB route.

The Rayner scrutinies were not the only initiative. In 1982 the Prime Minister launched the Financial Management Initiative (FMI). This initiative required government departments to establish clear objectives and well-established priorities, ensure that responsibilities of organisational sub-sections and key individuals were well defined and that personnel should be given the appropriate incentives and information to enable them to complete their responsibilities. Personal skills were also to be relevant for their responsibilities. The general purpose of the initiative was to push down responsibility to the level where adjustment of activities could affect costs. To do this, better information, especially about costs, was needed related to specific responsibilities.

When the FMI was launched each government department
was required to design an information system for senior
managers and ministers on a basis similar to the MINIS
system developed previously in the Department of the
Environment. This system took each major organisational
unit, specified its main activities, the objective of each
activity and the resources devoted to it. Ministers had
never had this type of information before. Departments
were also urged to develop performance measures - some
useful work has been done, but this side of things is not
so well developed.

Currently the Head of the Government Accountancy Service
is conducting a review of each department's budgetary
control system. This is seen to be very important for the
Treasury is unlikely to encourage decentralisation of
control until it can be very sure that budgetary control
structures are good.

At the outset of the FMI, there was a fair number of
sceptics of attempts to apply private sector approaches to
the management of efficiency and productivity to the
public sector. It was stated that expenditure was so
sensitive to political change or whim, that these would
swamp any gains in efficiency. Indeed the FMI has still
not achieved a state of full acceptance or application. It
is still unclear how the FMI will relate in the longer run
to the traditional governmental controls based on line-item
control, cash flow accounting and the separation of
receipts from related expenditure. Nevertheless, the FMI is
still continuing. It has raised many questions about control
over efficiency which, in itself, was valuable. It created
an awareness and debate. It is inconceivable that the FMI
will not leave its mark, and probably a substantial one, on

government control in the long run, even if the eventual
form and precise impact is still indeterminate. Also
significant steps have been taken by some government
departments in introducing more extensive and sophisticated
accounting and information systems (see Oates, 1986).

2. The National Health Service

In 1983, Sir Roy Griffiths, managing director of a large
retail supermarket chain, produced a report on the Health
Service which became very influential. The report
recommended that there should be a central management
board for the NHS, that general managers should be
appointed at regional, district and unit (ie hospital) level
and, in effect, the general principle of the FMI introduced
throughout the service (ie improved personal accountability,
clarification of roles, improved delegation along with more
detailed budgeting, etc). The report was implemented and
attempts began to manage the NHS using a style more like
a private sector business management approach (in contrast
to the 'consensus style' previously employed). General
managers were appointed because it was thought they could
manage - not because of experience in the Health Service.
Some general managers came from medicine, but equally
some were from industry and the armed forces.

As a result of this change, there is now considerable
activity taking place in the NHS, discussing new budgetary
systems. Issues addressed include the structure of the
budget - should it be based on the organisation structure
or on the medical speciality and at what level of detail.
Experimental work is also ongoing in trying to establish
flexible budgets for different case mixes. Similarly, there
is an upsurge of concern with developing performance

24

measures, information systems and regular performance appraisal of each element in the hierarchy by its immediate superior. Rayner type scrutinies have also been conducted in the NHS. While the major thrust has been on accountability, cost cutting and efficiency, there has, however, been a growing concern to improve the monitoring of service quality and now a reasonable number of health districts are undertaking their own experiments, ranging from highly structured questionnaire approaches to more informal discussions and idea development.

Certainly a lot has happened in recent years, but there are a few signs beginning to appear that the initial emphasis with the idea of getting a grip on efficiency was over-stressed. Very recently the Head of the Central Management Board resigned and various comments are appearing which challenge what are seen as the excesses of the private sector management approach in a sector where a consensus culture or management style has existed for years. An organisation culture cannot be dismissed by decree; it must itself be the subject of careful management if it is perceived in need of change. This is a very big task in an organisation which is amongst the largest employers in Europe with over 3/4 million staff. It seems to be in recognition of such matters that the Chairmanship of the Management Board has recently been taken over by the Minister of Health with Sir Roy Griffiths as Deputy Chairman who has, so it is reported, direct access to the Prime Minister. This change of balance recognises the importance of the combined need for political control to avoid alienation of the medical profession and management clout to ensure some change is achieved. Nevertheless, at the time of writing, much scepticism about the process still seems to be simmering just beneath the surface, but, even

if there is a change in political power at the next election
resulting in a generally different attitude towards public
spending, it is doubted if the process can be completely
reversed. The many experiments and developments should
continue to produce benefits, if only through legitimising
the process of challenging existing practices. A certain
amount of scepticism of the new approach is healthy, for it
enforces those seeking improvements to avoid ridiculous
claims in terms of increased efficiency or potential for
cost-cutting, but the sceptics must allow the innovators
space to experiment and raise questions about existing
practices.

3.   Local Authorities

The local authority network in the UK has consisted of
two tiers since the reorganisation of local government in
the mid-1970s. First, there are the County Councils and
then each County is divided into districts. Local
authorities receive approximately half of their operating
finance in the form of grants from central government and
raise the main part of the other half in the form of tax on
the notional value of property, called Rates. In most local
authorities capital expenditure is almost wholly debt
financed. UK local authorities are responsible for
Education, Social Services, Police, Housing and various
other services. They, therefore, represent very large
spending organisations.

Local authorities have been under severe financial pressure
since the oil crisis in 1974. Both Labour and Conservative
Governments have attempted to place a tighter control over
public expenditure in general and both parties have
attempted to exert stronger control over local authority

spending.

What would have been surprising to a Conservative supporter of the 1960s is how the Conservative Government has become more and more interventionist in attempting to exert control over local authorities. The classical political stance was the pressure for centralised coordinated control by the Socialists while the Conservatives were the party which encouraged local autonomy whereby local authorities were to manage their own affairs and provide services needed locally at costs the locality was prepared to afford. The need for tighter macro-economic management and the post-1979 thrust for efficiency has changed all that. There is little dispute now that the relationship between local government and central government is severely strained. We have learned that it needs very careful thought before one can pursue greater efficiency in a purely neutral way devoid of politics. It ought to be possible. It seems logical for everyone, from whatever political persuasion, to prefer more outputs from fewer inputs, but in pursuing that objective our experience indicates how easy it is to move from such a position of political neutrality into direct political confrontation on even basic constitutional issues. This is where the public sector is quite different from the private sector - it is extraordinarily difficult to keep campaigns for efficiency away from politics. I would like to come back to the issue again briefly, but first the various pressures for greater productivity in local government in recent years need to be reviewed.

First, from 1974, central government, both Conservative and Socialist, has gradually reduced the proportion of local government expenditure met by central government grant. This has put general pressure for economies upon local authorities although they were able, in principle, to maintain expenditure by increasing rates to make good the central government decreases in grant. In fact, initially, the decreased central government grant appeared to have little effect on total spending and so the Conservative Government introduced a more sophisticated grant mechanism. Under this new approach the Government provided expenditure targets for each authority determined for a base year and adjusted for allowable increases. If a local authority exceeded this target, the amount of central government grant otherwise payable was reduced by a penalty which eventually became very severe.

This development brought political opposition to the Conservative Government from Socialist local authorities and also some Conservative authorities. Some of the former category decided that the locality needed much more expenditure than the central government target and decided to go ahead and spend even if the whole central government grant was lost. These authorities had some very large increases in rates. On the other hand, quite a few Conservative local authorities protested that they had been trying to keep expenditure down and so, to provide a target upon a base year in which they had strictly controlled costs, treated them unfairly compared to other authorities who have spent more freely and so got an easier target. Detailed descriptions of these events are provided in Tomkins (1985).

These targets have now been abolished, but the Government has continued to use an estimate of what it thinks each local authority should spend (Grant Related Expenditure) and it still decreases the proportion of expenditure it is prepared to finance through central

government grant as an authority increases its expenditure
towards its GRE (if it was previously below it) or goes
above its GRE. After a given point above the GRE called
the threshold (10% above GRE), the penalty increases more
sharply.

Also, since the Rates Act, 1984, the Conservative
Government has taken steps to impose on top of the grant
system, a process whereby authorities who want to spend
(in spite of losses of central government grant), are
prevented from increasing local rates above an 'excessive'
level - this is called 'rate capping'. In 1985/86, 18 local
authorities were rate capped and 12 will be rate capped in
1986/87. This has lead to court action with most
authorities eventually levying a legal rate, but not without
considerable political tension and as much non-cooperation
and political advantage taken on the part of some
authorities as possible.

The Conservative Government's current declared position,
at least in terms of statements by the new Minister of the
Environment, is that it does want to give more autonomy
to local authorities, but it cannot do this without increased
accountability. The rating system, with rates being paid by
many without the vote (ie businesses) and only by property
owners, is seen as a system which encourages expenditure
because the burden falls on those without a vote or by no
means all the inhabitants of an area. The Government has,
therefore, indicated that it is seeking to replace the rating
system with a local taxation system where the burden falls
on all local inhabitants. It is hoped by that process local
authorities will be held more accountable for excessive
spending by the local electorate. At the time of writing
(November 1986) it has been proposed that Conservative

proposals for the reform of the Rating System will be included in the next Queen's speech, whether it is before or after the general election, and a Bill has already been produced for Scotland. This topic is further explored in Chapter 4. The Conservative Government has already, however, taken one interim step to improve accountability in the Rates Act 1984. From 1985/86 local authorities have had to consult local business interests prior to agreeing its budget and setting its rate. Not much seemed to happen in 1985/86, but it will be interesting to see whether such a piece of legislation 'has any teeth' from 1986/87 onwards.

Apart from this central government general financial pressure to induce greater efficiency, there have also been a number of specific steps taken directly aimed at increasing productivity.

Many local authorities have Direct Labour Organisations (DLOs). These are the authorities' own departments which may be involved in the construction of capital works (houses, minor roads, etc) or just maintenance work (again mainly of roads, houses and other authority establishments like schools and homes). The Conservative Government passed legislation providing that DLOs should have separate accounts and earn a return on investment of 5% (in current cost accounting terms) and that DLOs could not be awarded contracts by the local authority unless this was subject to competitive bidding. If the DLO could not achieve a 5% return on investment, it would be referred to the relevant Minister who might recommend that the particular DLO be closed down.

Since this DLO legislation, the Government has also introduced the 1985 Transport Act requiring companies to

be established, on a similar 'arm's length basis', to run
their transport undertakings. Also the Government is
considering whether to expand this 'detached' form of
public control into other forms of local authority services
such as refuse collection, street cleaning, maintenance of
parks, etc.

The main philosophy seems to be that there should be
public sector oversight of the provision of those services,
but the provider of the services should be placed in a
market competitive position in order to stimulate greater
efficiency and productivity. Without researching the
question thoroughly, informal contacts with local
government do indicate that the new DLO legislation has
certainly increased awareness of local authority DLO
managers on the need to be as efficient as their
equivalents in the private sector. There are, however,
stories of large private sector organisations being able to
offer 'loss leader' tenders as the local authority work was
not their main source of sales and this represented unfair
competition on the DLOs which, of course, could not do
that and achieve the required real rate of return of 5%.
But while this may seem unfair to DLO managers, it may
be indicative that they are unable to achieve desirable
economies of scale and so, however unfair it may seem to
be, should be disbanded or encouraged to combine across
several local authority regions in order to achieve the
scale needed.

Closely related in philosophy to this development regarding
DLOs has been the adoption of a policy of 'contracting
out' the provision of some types of services. Quite a
number (though still by far the minority) of local
authorities have disbanded their own service provision and

31

invited private tenders for the work. This has largely related to well structured tasks like various forms of maintenance, refuse collection, etc where quality of performance can readily be assessed. A recent study by the London Business School indicates that savings of about 20% have been achieved by local authorities contracting out refuse collection and that, if all authorities followed the example of the few, there are total potential savings of £80 million per annum (Domberger, Meadowcroft and Thompson, 1986).

Perhaps the most significant effort at improving productivity in local government has come through the creation of the Audit Commission.[4,5] Prior to 1979 local authorities were audited by a section of the Central

---

[4] Changes were also introduced into audit at national level with the National Audit Act 1983. This has not, however, been emphasised here as it came about to a large extent through a back-bencher's luck in the ballot to introduce legislation. The Government had considered new legislation was unnecessary - see Keemer, 1985, Chapter 4 and some further comments in Chapter 4 of this text.

[5] The Audit Commission does not, of course, have jurisdiction in Scotland, but its efforts in improving 'management auditing' are worthy of study by accountants everywhere.

Government's Department of the Environment. Mrs Thatcher's first Government established a new independent Audit Commission and charged it to take over the audit staff from the Department of the Environment and to place far more emphasis on value-for-money auditing instead of the previous domination of regularity auditing. A director was brought in from McKinsey and Company to run the Commission and, contrary to some earlier fears, the Commission has shown itself to be independent of the central government, sometimes criticising central government arrangements in support of local government.

The basic thrust of the Audit Commission has been to conduct a number of studies in order to establish 'best practice' with regard to specific local authority services or operations. All auditors working under the Commission's direction were then required to compare each authority's performance against these comparative statistics and explain any differences, always looking for opportunities to find savings. In addition, auditors were encouraged to develop their own efficiency audits (ie not designed by the Audit Commission).

In addition to these efficiency audits, the Commission introduced a new audit approach (developed by McKinsey and Company) by which all auditors were to examine the total management arrangements of each authority.

When the Audit Commission was established, it was also required to contract out a large number of local authority audits to private sector accountancy firms. The object seemed to be, once more, to provide some private sector competition for the public sector auditors and, indeed, the head of the Audit Commission has lost no opportunity to

encourage competition between the public and private
sector auditors.

There is little doubt that the establishment of the Audit
Commission has been a success. It has identified
possibilities for significant savings, although it is not clear
how much of these 'possibilities' have become 'realities'.
One remembers the experience of the Rayner scrutinies and
so hesitates before claiming too much. The Commission
has, however, created a new climate and attitude towards
improving efficiency. Moreover, by distancing itself from
central government policy and trying to offer its service to
local authorities 'as a helping hand', it seems to have
overcome many earlier prophesies of resistance.

The Commission quite properly and wisely commenced its
first year of operation with a focus upon improving the
efficiency of well structured tasks - these were tasks
which could be defined clearly and inputs and outputs
measured without undue difficulty. It has also, as stated
above, been very innovative in establishing audits of
overall management arrangements. It has not, however, yet
been able to do much in the way of evaluating the
effectiveness of local authority services. One can measure
the improvement of input-output ratios (eg teacher to
graduating student ratios), but it is quite a different
matter to place a value on those teachers' work. Did the
graduating students really have the skills society needs?
Could they have acquired them without the teachers?
Much more fundamental issues are raised when considering
whether educational expenditure constitutes value for
money. There are some signs that the Audit Commission is
beginning to move into such issues and it is at that level
that it will have its greatest difficulty in evaluating service

'productivity'. At least the Commission seems to be making the right sort of statements. Evaluation of effectiveness, rather than the narrower concept of efficiency, will require cooperation of auditors with those who understand and run the specialist services. Such cooperation will not be forthcoming if the task is approached in an aggressive manner which seeks to lay blame or find fault. So far the Audit Commission has been fairly successful at acting with local authorities to seek improvements and so the correct basis for moving on to more complex questions of effectiveness has been laid. Moreover, the Commission's recent handbook 'Performance review in Local Government' makes a strong and useful move in the direction of addressing effectiveness issues. One should also not be too critical. The Commission can only be expected to operate within existing bounds of knowledge and much research remains to be done in testing approaches to reviewing effectiveness.

This climate of relative cooperation is in contrast to that between local authorities and central government where, it was stated earlier, relations are strained. There the quest for economy and efficiency has spilled over into direct political confrontation in some areas. The upshot of this has been the introduction of legislation which has resulted in the abolition of the Greater London Council and the large Metropolitan County Councils. These were all Socialist dominated and their responsibilities have been given to smaller authorities. The Conservative Government argued that these large local authorities were incurring excessive expenditure and were needlessly large bureaucracies. The authorities themselves claimed their perceived democratic rights to spend as they saw fit for their localities. In fact both sides did not hesitate from making political mileage over these events.

To repeat the message obtained earlier, what might seem to management scientists and consultants to be a political neutral quest for increased efficiency in the public sector can, so easily, become distorted and reinterpreted in the political arena. If one is not careful the political right comes to be seen as the only party concerned with efficiency while also appearing uncaring. In contrast the political left claims it alone cares for the quality of public service and is prepared to spend more on them. Surely, this is a misunderstanding of both political viewpoints. While the political right and left may have different views of the sort of society we need, both must have some concern for improved efficiency and improved quality of service. We do not have such a bounty of resources available to us that either side can ignore either aspect of value-for-money. Productivity gains will not be achieved in the public sector unless great care is taken to remove such steps from the political battlefield. Doing so using a neutral buffer organisation like the Audit Commission seems to be one way of minimising the difficulty. On the other hand, political ideologies often reflect the interests of political constituencies. The practical effects of cost cutting and increased efficiency may not affect the constituencies of different political parties in the same way. Hence, it may be impossible to obtain complete political neutrality on some issues of productivity. This point will also be addressed later in this book.

4.   The Universities

The universities are not strictly part of the public sector for statistical purposes, but their nature requires their

36

inclusion in the book. The universities have not been exempt from this pressure for increased productivity. Moreover, the need for control over public expenditure has coincided with a long-term trend which is about to result in a dramatic fall in the number of persons of school leaving age. The natural tendency has, therefore, been to want to cut the size of the university sector. This has been conducted by two separate reviews of the University Grants Committee. In 1981 the UGC announced cuts in grants to universities which averaged 17% but which was over 40% in some cases. With 60 - 70% of university expenditure on staff, strains were imposed upon the university system as many were encouraged to leave. More recently, the UGC has just completed a more thorough review of each university department's research record and placed university departments in different categories of performance. This categorisation together with consideration of other factors, such as the efficiency of the university in terms of costs per student, led to differential cuts of grants to universities. All universities have suffered some more cuts in real terms, but some rather more than others.

Cuts in spending do not, as repeatedly argued, necessarily increase either efficiency or effectiveness. Recognising this the Government established the Jarratt Committee (1985) to investigate the management process of universities. The report was critical of universities' lack of clear objectives and a goal orientated management. Moreover, the Government is now trying to link the question of increasing academic salaries to questions of personal performance evaluation in terms of research and teaching, the removal of the right to tenure of one's academic position and other efficiency matters.

There is no doubt that universities have, as a result of these pressures, become more efficient if by efficient we mean the production of students at lower real costs to the State. Most universities have had to be far more active at seeking work from the private sector simply to avoid bankruptcy. It could be argued that this is also healthy; the closer the link between universities and the private sector, the more likely the former will serve industries' needs in research and provision of students with the right skills. Equally, there is currently a strained relationship between the central government and the university system (or most of it). There are many fears that the quests for both efficiency and private sector contracts will so fundamentally change universities, the management structures and systems of accountability that traditional academic values and performance will be threatened. It is not yet clear where this series of events will end. In so far as one does need to question the purpose and existence of the university system occasionally, the developments seem healthy. Unfortunately, it is very difficult to carry on a rational debate about such issues when we have the current polarisation of political views in the UK with, as described earlier, one main party having the image of seeking nothing but efficiency and the other one of simply wanting to increase public spending. Surely neither is true, but the political perspectives and images set the climate within which we are supposed to be having a rational consideration of the role of universities. Within such a climate it sometimes does not pay participants in the struggle to present too rational or neutral a case why they should suffer contraction. Also, in the case of education at all levels, it seems natural that staff should be less than enthusiastic over reform when they see

38

themselves, rightly or wrongly, grossly underpaid. Once
again one cannot achieve major change in large sectors of
the economy without setting the right climate for change.

5.   The Nationalised Industries

The final category of the UK public sector to be addressed
is that of the nationalised industries (ie electricity, gas,
coal, rail, etc). These industries are state owned, but
given very broad terms of reference and the Board of each
industry is left to run its own industry. In 1980, however,
the Competition Act (S.11) gave the Trade Secretary power
to make reference to the Monopolies and Mergers
Commission on questions of efficiency, abuse of monopoly
power and related matters. The Commission has focused a
lot of effort on reviewing investment appraisal and
criticised quite severely practices in identification of
investment options, forecasting cash flows and risk
analysis. In terms of financial control, the Commission
advocates pushing down responsibility for costs to the
lowest level in line with the FMI and expects to see
production planning and incentive schemes based upon
standard lines for each task.

Where matters are referred to the Commission, detailed
investigations are made sometimes by using management
consultants. Evidence is then heard in public hearings and
agreement is both rigorous and vigorous. The general
approach adopted by the Commission is to investigate
modes of operation rather than detailed events and it has
established 'norms' of best practice with respect to
management structures, systems, financial planning and
control, investment appraisal and employee practices.
There is now a series of reports dealing with such issues

in different nationalised bodies covering rail, water, electricity, aviation, bus transport, hydro-electricity, and further reports are due on steel and the postal services.

While the Monopolies and Mergers Commission worked away at its efficiency reviews without over-much publicity, much more public and press attention focused on the process of privatisation of the nationalised industries. The Conservative Government decided that it would be far more of a stimulus to make nationalised industries subject to the pressures of the stock market and, where possible, product competition. As each industry reached a healthy enough position, it would be privatised and, following this policy, over 50% of British Telecom was sold in November 1984 and British Gas followed soon after.

There are, however, as discussed in Chapter 1, grounds for debate as to where the dividing line between the private and public sectors should come. While privatised industries may have a majority private sector shareholding, natural monopolies still need regulation to prevent these industries using their monopoly power to create excessive profits. Questions of public accountability still arise, even if these industries are privately owned. It is also unclear what attitude a Conservative Government would take if a privatised British Coal, British Steel, British Rail or Electricity Boards faced another miners' strike. That strike was without question defeated because the Government was able to back these nationalised industries despite its claim not to have directly intervened in the dispute.

Reflecting on the Experience

With the oil crises of 1974 and 1979, there was unquestionably the need in the UK to exercise constraint and encourage improved efficiency. Either main political party would have found itself forced into this position whether it liked it or not. It has also been shown, in outline, how there has been a range of different reactions to the general economic situation. There have been straightforward pressures through simply cutting funding from central government sources, penalties for overspending, efficiency reviews and scrutinies, new audit bodies with an emphasis on encouraging value-for-money, new information and budgetary systems, pressures for improved accountability and so on. In other words a frontal attack has been made on the question of public sector productivity using a variety of means. Unquestionably, all these approaches have yielded some benefits. There have been large cost savings and there has been a greater interest in seeking greater efficiency. Also, there is no doubt that anyone working in the public sector - from local authority to a university - will have noted a major shift in management attitude and culture. Having said that, various issues are apparent from this review that deserve more attention if public sector management is to be further improved.

First, while the failure of over-bureaucratic systems like PPBS and ZBB had been widely recognised, the calls for improvements in public sector management are replete with the specification of overall organisation objectives, with the analysis of those objectives into separable sub-tasks with responsibility and budget/cost accountability forced down to the lowest level. The systematisation of the Rayner scrutinies may lead to an institutionalisation of the process which robs them of their innovativeness and success. This is not to say that specification of objectives and responsibility accounting are undesirable, but

41

there is a remarkable lack of recognition in the public sector
management literature that this 'control paradigm' is only one
way of looking at any organisation. Recognition, in a more
explicit way, of alternative perceptions of what public sector
organisations are may enable us to move beyond the general
exhortations to achieve objectives and control to them.

Next, it is quite clear that the major emphasis over the last
seven years has been to improve <u>efficiency</u> (that is an
improvement in the input-output ratio) and more often it seems
that the Government was more concerned with fewer inputs
rather than more outputs. Efficiency is not, however,
synonymous with effectiveness. Ultimately one must relate
spending to the value derived from the outputs in terms of
benefits to society. An improved input-output ratio has only
limited value if we are not sure that we should be doing this
activity at all or that it could not be done in an entirely
different way. There is growing awareness now that management
concern must move beyond efficiency questions. Local authorities
are becoming more conscious of the 'provision of service', health
districts are experimenting with ways of improving the quality of
service, even the Audit Commission now seems prepared to build
upon its basis of efficiency studies to grapple some of the more
complex issues on effectiveness. There is also a need, therefore,
in this book to consider how effectiveness may be evaluated.

In addition, increased efficiency may not even decrease costs
unless managed carefully. One simple example will suffice based
on the health district in the author's home town, Bath. A major
effort was made to reduce the waiting list for orthopaedic
treatment in a hospital. The effect was a great success: the
waiting list was reduced from 2,400 persons to 1,500 persons
through greater productivity. The increased output increased the
orthopaedic department costs by £160,000 and drew money from

other priority areas. Of course, the increased productivity was beneficial; the drop in the visiting time would even contribute to most patients' ideas of effectiveness, but this example shows the danger of a myopic focus on only one aspect of the organisation's activity. There is a need to see the linkages between systems and competing claims. One immediately comes right back to the need for a more comprehensive view of the organisation which is probably what Sir Robin Ibbs felt on taking over the 'Rayner scrutinies'. It seems that the issue of the need for overall coordination and control versus the requirements for initiative in improving efficiency and effectiveness will need to be one key theme in this book.

There is also another, much broader, sense in which it needs to be recognised that increased efficiency is not necessarily the same as cost cutting. Initially, there is no doubt that the Conservative Government was pledged to reducing public expenditure, and yet examining public expenditure as a whole there has been a 10% increase in real terms between 1979/80 and 1984/85. Despite the considerable activity to improve efficiency described in outline in this chapter, the Government did not achieve its main purpose of cutting the size of the public sector. It has achieved considerable reductions in the areas of support to trade and industry (-32%) and in housing (-55.1%) and one or two small reductions elsewhere, but these decreases have been swamped by increased in Defence (+23%), Law and Order (+31%), Social Security (+28%) and Health and Personal Social Services (+17%). Even leaving out of the calculation the considerable resources devoted to supporting the unemployed, there is still no overall real decrease in public expenditure. Similarly, at local government level, spending has increased by over 10% in real terms between 1979/80 and 1984/85. (If rent rebates and housing is excluded the real level of expenditure is largely unchanged.) Neither centrally nor locally, therefore, has the aggregate 'volume' of expenditure been reduced.

No political evaluation or view is intended here in respect of
whether an increase or decrease in public expenditure is
desirable; the point being made is this. The vast majority of the
informed population and those working in the public sector are
aware of the wide range of changes described in this chapter and
look for evidence of success. These developments have, however,
all emphasised the improvement of operational efficiency. It
should have been forseeable that improvements in operational
efficiency, most valuable as they are cumulatively over the longer
run, were unlikely to yield large savings in the short run
(although one can also debate whether six years is the short
run). The £300 million probably saved by the Rayner scrutinies
is only about 1/4 of 1% of public expenditure. Similarly the £80
million apparently saved in local government by contracting out,
while a very welcome saving, is less than 1/2 of 1% of local
government spending. Even the full 'potential' saving of £400
million is little more than 1.5%. A significant reduction of public
expenditure was a strategic question requiring a more
fundamental reappraisal of options. By emphasising the
operational efficiency level, one may wonder whether there was a
fundamental lack of appreciation of the difference between
operations and strategy. Strategic change needs different tools
to those required for improving operational efficiency.

The view expressed in the previous paragraph is, however,
probably an unjust assessment of the Government's ability to
think analytically. The more reasonable interpretation is that, in
addition to developing the wide range of steps to improve
operational efficiency, the Government did attempt to think
strategically. There is evidence of this in the case of the cuts
in spending in Trade and Industry and significant increases in
other areas. As regards the overall objective of cutting public

44

sector expenditure, therefore, it seems more charitable to infer that, on studying the consequences, the Government quietly modified its main objective from 'overall cuts' to 'no substantial overall increase'. Nevertheless, the experience provides a first class example for this book of the need to consider carefully whether the tools to achieve ends are the appropriate ones. This also needs to be pursued a little later in the book.

This review of UK experiences also indicates the difference between analysis and achievement. Only a proportion of the savings identified by the Rayner scrutinies have been achieved. One suspects the same for the savings possibilities identified by the Audit Commission. Examination is, therefore, also needed of the question of whether less attention to analysis and more to implementation would bring bigger benefits. Moreover, a scrutiny by one or two bright individuals may lead to a rational analysis for change, but people who have power and control have to be convinced. The management consultant who does not recognise organisation politics may end up having most of his reports left aside. This problem is especially prevalent in the public sector where there is, at present, no clear bottom line accountability.

In addition to organisation politics, this review has shown how important party politics can be in promoting or resisting change. None of the changes described in this chapter have been achieved without considerable political tension. Perhaps this is inevitable. When attempting such a major shift in attitudes and an entrenched public sector culture, perhaps the only way is to be tough, uncompromising and, indeed, encourage confrontation in order to demonstrate determination that things will change. Mrs Thatcher has been successful in doing that and I doubt if she was very surprised at the reactions she got - either across the party political divide or the central - local government boundary. The question then arises as to whether such change could have been achieved without a sizeable political majority and what happens if it disappears at the next election, or if there is a hung parliament? Will this alter how one views public sector management? On the other hand, perhaps cultures can be changed without dominant power. If so, public sector managers and consultants need to consider how this can be done.

Finally, underlying all the pressure for increased efficiency over the last seven years lies the concern for improved public accountability. While the recent focus has been on accountability for efficient performance and a Labour Government might be more concerned with employees welfare and consumer service, all main political parties seem to want increased accountability. This then provides another major element which needs to be addressed in a discussion of public sector management and probably provides a marked difference between the public and private sectors.

This discussion of events since 1979 and a certain amount of reflection on them, therefore, has led to the identification of a number of areas where further thought is needed in order to improve public sector management. Some brief consideration to each of these areas will be given in the rest of this book. First, the questions of effectiveness and accountability are important and distinct enough to be dealt with separately. The remaining range of issues (the nature of control in the public sector, the distinction between strategy and operations, being aware of linkages within the system, improving implementation not just analysis and changing organisational cultures) will then all be addressed together in the last chapter devoted to managing change in public sector organisations. It must be stressed, however, that each of these topics would provide the basis for a book and so only outline treatment can be presented in this brief publication. Moreover, there are no panaceas. New directions and emphasis may be suggested but <u>no-one</u> knows <u>THE</u> answer to these issues. The ideas are, therefore, offered as suggestions as to where consultants and academics might usefully focus their own thought and practice development.

3   CLOSING THE EFFECTIVENESS GAP

The UK debate over improved management in the public sector has focused upon management processes. There have been calls for setting clear objectives, improving accountability for actions and improving operational efficiency, but the most basic ingredient required has been missing. How can clear objectives be formulated and how can clear accountability be devised unless there is an equally clear definition of effectiveness? Even the most sophisticated attempt to date to review an organisation's total management system, that is the Audit Commission's proposal to use the McKinsey 7-S framework (see The Audit Commission Handbook and Peters and Waterman, 1982) assumes that effectiveness can be judged in a reasonably clear way. The framework asks if the authority has a clear vision of where it is going, and whether the strategies, skills, systems, etc are consistent with that end. All of this is meaningless if it is impossible to decide when a public service is being effective and when it isn't. Without this information it is impossible to form any rational judgment over priorities and hence visions and strategies.

As stated before, the Audit Commission and indeed other public sector auditors and managers were probably wise to focus on improving operational efficiency first. To have delved straight into the complexities of effectiveness evaluation in the education or health services would have left the various agencies wide open to the charge of being too impractical, with such a loss of credibility initially; this would have built no base from which more sophisticated evaluations could proceed. Hence, we have seen an overwhelming focus upon the evaluation of well-structured tasks where output is definable and measurable with relative ease and where there is not too much debate over what effectiveness is.

There are signs, however, that the time has now come to move to more complex issues. It has become recognised that there is a limit to the total input reductions which can be achieved on public spending by improving efficiency on structured tasks which are often relatively minor areas of public spending. Also, the subtle changes in Government policy which recently tends to give the impression of some relaxation on public spending, and also the possible change in Government at the next election, are themselves stimuli to move beyond the narrower efficiency and cost-cutting perspective. At last, therefore, we may be moving into the era when the core issues of public spending may be addressed. Namely, how do we set about evaluating and monitoring the effectiveness of public sector service. Effectiveness here is taken to mean the value which society desires from given inputs and outputs of a particular public service.

Current Developments in Terms of Improving Effectiveness

Several developments are occurring which aim to focus more on effectiveness. One approach focuses upon the derivation of performance measures and, in essence, is trying to extend the notion of control through responsibility accounting. The reason that it is difficult to evaluate effectiveness, it is argued, is simply that we have not yet developed measures for it. It is assumed that intelligent people with due application can develop such measures. Thus one sees the retention of the basic objectives-plan-monitor-control approach to management; all that is needed are the new measures.

One problem in discussing the question is that the discussion on performance measures so easily confuses a range of different ideas on comparative statistics whether one is concerned with comparisons of actual with estimated figures or comparisons across similar public bodies. There must be a distinction between a comparison of statistics relating to inputs, comparisons of input-output ratios and the achievement of social ends.

Comparisons of inputs may raise interesting questions which lead to investigations which do raise matters relating to effectiveness. Comparisons of input-output ratios address questions of productive efficiency and may be related to increased effectiveness. Nevertheless, those performance measures are not, per se, adequate for the complete assessment of effectiveness.

Despite considerable effort in both the UK and abroad to devise performance measures, the results are not very encouraging for this approach to evaluating effectiveness. Pollitt (1986) reviewed three recent proposals for performance indicators (Bexley's Annual Review, The CIPFA (1984 version) performance indicators for Education, and the DHSS/NHS indicators). He found that overwhelmingly the indicators focused upon the measurement of efficiency (ie input-output ratios). Also, the CIPFA Education indicators which were credited with 12% being related to effectiveness, are really no more than possible question raisers about social impact rather than directly focusing on effectiveness in a particular authority. How could they be? The indicators are offered as general indicators for all education authorities (CIPFA, 1986). Some statistics are suggested which would help a local education authority establish 'a local profile' of the context within which it has to conduct its educational activities, but that is really no more than an information sub-set (though an important one) of that required for the policy making process. It does not begin to suggest what would be an effective policy for that locality. Moreover, Mayston (1985) states that the massive number of performance indicators developed from the USA Federal Government Productivity Measurement Programme are not widely used and so the problem is not uniquely British.

On the other hand, it is easy to dismiss these attempts to find suitable performance indicators too quickly. Appendix I shows, as just one illustration, what can be done in the public sector. That appendix shows a set of indicators currently being proposed for use in universities. Such a set of information would be useful if it is used properly as focusing upon key questions to debate in the formulation of policy to improve effectiveness. It is obvious that the key effectiveness questions (namely the 'value added' to the student through his educational experience and the 'value added' to society by the research performed) are not covered by the indicators prescribed. Also there may be the danger that the reporting of research income itself becomes the goal rather than the pursuit of quality (and cost effective) research. Nevertheless, all numerical performance measures, in either the private or public sector, may be mis-used. The measures pre-suppose some intelligence and sensitivity in their use. When new performance indicator systems are introduced this may, of course, imply that there is a need to educate those using the measures; perhaps even to educate those that constructed them in terms of demonstrating unforeseen effects the measures may have. Despite all this, it seems clear that those responsible for managing universities will gain a better insight to university department and academic performance with such information rather than without it.

Also, the Audit Commission (1986) has recently published details of key indicators and key questions for auditors and local authority members to ask to review policies with respect to all major local authority services. This is to be welcomed as a key step forward and not dismissed as just another set of statistical indicators. The very act of thinking about the use and limitations of such measures can lead to insights about effectiveness. The essential requirement is the assumption of some intelligence and sophistication in interpreting the numbers and answers to the questions.

Performance indicators, therefore, can be useful. They are useful if used carefully to raise key questions for further enquiry and debate. Moreover, if one wishes to gain an overview of a total activity, it seems inevitable that some summary statistics will be needed. Indicators, therefore, have a key role to play in the evaluation of effectiveness, but the evaluation can never be complete by relying on indicators alone. Where performance relates to social activities which have no clear 'production functions' for converting inputs into unambiguously beneficial social impacts (and this applies to most of the public sector) something further is needed.

What do We Mean by Effectiveness and How Can We Assess It?

Now that 'effectiveness' is becoming the relevant buzz-word for the next few years, it is very important to consider carefully what it might mean. Without conceptual clarity as to what it is, we shall see a flurry of activity with little real achievement. Everyone knows that effectiveness relates to social impact, but that is relatively useless for the practicing manager or policy-maker. Moreover, commonly used definitions are often of little help. One of the leading accounting firms has used the following definition:

> "Effectiveness may be defined as how well a programme or activity is achieving its stated objectives, its defined goals (eg targets/market share) or other intended effects."

The trouble with that definition is that it begs the question in that it assumes that we know what effectiveness is, otherwise, the objectives and goals could not have been set. In addition, the definition only refers to intended effects. No doubt the Soviets did not intend that the Chernobyl accident would occur, but it was a very relevant matter in evaluating their effectiveness. Of course, it could be argued in such an extreme case that there was an implicit intention that such an accident should not occur but, in less dramatic situations, one cannot rule

52

out unexpected occurrences, some with beneficial and some with undesirable effects, even if the intended and stated goals are perfectly achieved. So one is left with the conclusion that the effectiveness of a public service must be judged on the basis of all intended and unintended effects. Also, one must establish a clear idea of what an effective service is before establishing objectives and goals. Specification of goals involves choice of options and the most preferred options cannot be selected unless their attractiveness in terms of effectiveness is known.

The current move to focus on effectiveness has led to a number of experiments in establishing consumer needs or local taxpayer views. In the local authority sphere Cleveland County Council has regularly surveyed local opinion since 1974 to gain views on its services. Various other local authorities have followed suit more recently. Also, in the Health Service, a number of experiments are being carried out in order to identify consumers views and, of course, in other spheres, consumer councils have existed for many years. Several points, however, need to be made. First, there needs to be a distinction between consumers and the taxpayers. In a local authority, for example, those benefiting from local education, social service or other services are not necessarily those paying the rates. The views of the two sets of persons may, therefore, be in direct opposition to each other which will itself establish some sort of ambiguity over the question of what effectiveness is. Next, there may be the tendency for consumers to look on such surveys as a complaints system. If public sector managers are using consumer surveys as the basis of evaluating service effectiveness, they will want to identify general features. This may leave individual consumers frustrated with apparent lack of attention to their own issues. In fact, the author was present at a recent seminar where an interesting exchange took place in relation to the role consumers' representatives took with regard to a nationalised industry. One said that consumers always wanted to reduce the debate to trivia not associated with strategic questions, while the consumer side said that management would not let the consumers influence strategy such that it was forced to try to express its views via a 'complaints style' of case. Finally, asking the consumer also pre-supposes that the consumer has enough knowledge to provide a meaningful answer. The consumer may well be able to answer how effective a hospital is at calling him for examination, avoiding him spending too long in the waiting room, being civil at reception or comfortable in the ward. Can he, however, properly evaluate the effectiveness of the provision of medical service, bearing in mind the available resources? The consumer, therefore, may have useful information inputs to make, but that is not in itself the evaluation of effectiveness from the service viewpoint.

With an even narrower focus, there have also been efforts recently to improve relationships at the client-staff interface. This seems to be following the route of obvious parallels in the private sector: the well-known advertising of American Express or Barclays Bank emphasised their friendly approach to customers. Once more this may offer a valuable contribution to increased effectiveness in service delivery, not only in terms of immediate relationships, but also in terms of encouraging better communication and feedback from the consumer. On the other hand, a smiling doctor or nurse is not contributing much to effectiveness in telling the patient that he or she has to wait for months for an operation.

From even this brief discussion, effectiveness then seems to have various facets which make it quite different from efficiency. An efficiency calculation assumes a clearly defined output. Effectiveness, in contrast, seems to involve all effects, whether intended or not, and needs inputs from a variety of sources. Managers, consumers, professional service providers and general employees all seem to have a part to play in the determination of what effectiveness is. Once one admits the relevance of different groups, one must allow for the emergence of competing interests. Indeed, even within well-spread groups of doctors, rate-payers, patients etc it is likely that competing views will emerge. It is, however, the responsibility of some set of top policy makers to decide what the main strategic goals of the service shall be. At that level the main issues must be identified. A general approach for handling such a process is suggested by Guba and Lincoln (1981).

The main thrust of the Guba and Lincoln approach to effectiveness evaluation, is to recognise the plurality of the concept already described and the need to identify key issues which need attention. The organisation is assumed to have an existence and a current level of service provision. There is no need, for most purposes, to try to establish global objectives relating to the raison d'etre of the service. A pragmatic approach will identify main current issues and plan to deal with them.

The effectiveness analysis should start, therefore, not with management's goals, but with the identification of all main stakeholders who have an interest in the service. Each type of stakeholder will then be sampled to discover what are the major concerns of that group. These concerns will then be assessed to see whether they are simply the cause of mis-information or truly significant in terms of identifying something which may need rectification. Only the latter are defined as 'issues'. Usually there will be some issues on which there is general consensus and these can be first-line candidates for action subject to resource constraints. Usually, there will also be issues which represent conflicting interests. The Guba and Lincoln standpoint is that such conflicting positions arise because of conflicting sets of values held by the opposing parties. It should, therefore, be the effectiveness evaluator's task to identify

55

these underlying values and make them explicit. This will not resolve the conflict for the top policy-makers, but it will enable them to address the underlying values involved and match them against their own. The idea is that this process will enable more informed choice of issues to be resolved.

Obviously, political concerns will never be removed from choice in the public sector and policy-makers may simply want to disregard certain groups' views. This cannot, however, be used as an argument to discredit completely such an effectiveness analysis for that would assume that top management would never listen to anyone else and always have adequate information. There must always be some realm within which they need information, views and participation to some degree from different interested parties. Political views may constrain the field within which the search for effectiveness takes place, but there is still much scope for reviewing effectiveness within any political viewpoint.

Viewed in this way, effectiveness becomes a pragmatic concept and the pursuit of effectiveness analysis becomes feasible. Moreover, it becomes quite clear where management's objectives fit into the pursuit of effectiveness and where they do not. Effectiveness, in terms of specific concerns and issues, need to be defined and evaluated first. From that management's goals are formulated, action implemented and monitored to assess the achievement of goals. In addition, at relevant periods, concerns and issues must be reviewed again to capture both intended and unintended effects to see whether management's goals need revision. There are, in other words, two interacting control loops indicated in Figure 3.1. The concept seems simple; almost obvious. But in that case why is so much of the debate about effectiveness even still couched in terms of achievement of management's goals? The point is well made by Scriven (1986),

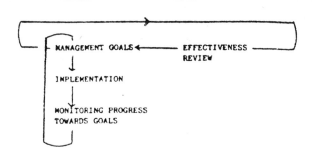

FIGURE 3.1   THE DUAL CONTROL LOOPS RELATING TO EFFECTIVENESS AND
ACHIEVEMENT OF GOALS

who literally shocked the evaluation research community several years ago in proposing goal free evaluations:

"If social scientists had spent more time thinking about the kind of product evaluation on which they based many of their own most important consumer purchases, we might have been spared the long period in which it was, and still is, supposed that checking programs to see if they met their goals was the main aim and only proper concern of evaluation."

The Guba and Lincoln approach, therefore, eschews trying ito develop philosophical meanings of effectiveness. It is a practical approach focusing on <u>specific</u> concerns and related very much to a practicing manager's sense of reality.   It deserves to be considered widely throughout the public sector and public sector managers and their advisers are urged to experiment with it.

The Guba approach is not, however, the only approach to effectiveness review. There is a considerable volume of literature in the USA related to effectiveness evaluation in education, health and social services.

Very broadly these approaches can be divided between (i) the 'scientific', that is to say based upon systems concepts with an emphasis on neutral performance indicators, and (ii) the 'naturalistic', that is approaches which do not purport to measure effectiveness in any unique or neutral way, but intend to facilitate an understanding of the situation faced. Guba and Lincoln make it clear that they consider themselves in the latter category. Alternative 'naturalistic' approaches to that of Guba and Lincoln might involve the preparation of case studies from which lessons about effectiveness can be learned, development of quasi-judicial courts to argue the case (like public hearings over planning applications), or establishment of expert connoisseurs of the service (presumably school inspectors are supposed to be in the latter vein, but there is scope for a more rigorous integration of such a role into the management process).

Space prevented a full analysis and so the author has exercised his own bias in focusing on the Guba and Lincoln approach. Readers seeking more may refer to Grimwood and Tomkins, (1986) or Madaus, et al (1983) for more depth where evaluators representing each major method describe their own viewpoints.

The Relative Roles of Management and Auditors in Effectiveness Evaluation

Attractive though the Guba and Lincoln methodology is, one must not confuse its simplicity with ease of application. Although the concepts are simple in their approach, it would take a considerable effort to implement it thoroughly across all public services. One must then consider whether such an effectiveness review is itself cost-effective - especially if one also follows Guba and Lincoln in avoiding the use of questionnaires in favour of interviewing. Also one is reminded of the experience in widespread effectiveness evaluations in the USA and the growing scepticism of whether they produce value-for-money. Schmidt (1983) says 'that most evaluation studies are read by few people and acted upon by even fewer'. Also Swarz (1980) argues that 'an enormous investment (in evaluation studies) has failed to yield significant benefits'. Taking heed of these warnings, it is, therefore, advocated that external auditors do not embark upon a widespread practice of Guba-style audits. If this approach is to prove useful, it will be so if management sets up a periodic service review of the Guba-type. It is after all management that should be trying to achieve an effective service in the first place. The auditor's role should then be to see that such effectiveness reviews are conducted and that, when conducted, they are performed rigorously. Elsewhere (Tomkins, forthcoming), it is argued how it is quite feasible to think of establishing a set of audit standards relating quite directly to public sector effectiveness audits. There are already some instances of such a move in the USA.

This brief review of effectiveness, therefore, urges public sector managers and auditors alike to cease discussing these matters as generalities and recognise that more rapid progress is likely to be made by focusing on specific issues than in vague exhortations about value-for-money. One needs to beware, however, setting up costly systems and reviews because it appears rational to do so. To avoid excessive costs, effectiveness reviews should probably be pursued selectively and periodically by the organisations delivering the service, or consultants assisting them. Auditors should also become more sophisticated. The Audit Commission 7-S type of organisational analysis could, for example, incorporate a consideration of how well the 'corporate vision' is based upon a review of effectiveness and whether the review of effectiveness was conducted according to appropriate methodological and ethical standards. This latter task would be an exciting task for the auditing profession and one in which the key institutes should be involved.

At our current state of knowledge, a two-pronged attack upon effectiveness evaluation is, therefore, proposed. For routine monitoring of organisation units as a whole, the chief executive does need key indicators. Efforts should be devoted to constructing a parsimonious list (see Rockhart, 1979) of indicators likely to cause some investigation where performance is significantly inadequate. With the introduction of such indicators, it is possible that they would soon cease to create much debate. Their very existence, reinforced by knowledge of possible chief executive sanctions, would induce routine compliance with performance as measured. It is important, therefore, to probe effectiveness at a level which such global indicators cannot detect. A Guba and Lincoln stakeholder analysis seems to be a front runner for a methodology to do this. Hence, for example, a University Vice-Chancellor might not just monitor research income, but from time to time canvass the views of research sponsors on the quality and value of the research performed. It seems clear, at least to this author, that as effectiveness evaluations develop in the UK, we shall see the emergence of systems which have both overall quantitative indicators and largely qualitative micro-studies of specific issues - the one approach will complement the other.

APPENDIX I   POSSIBLE PERFORMANCE INDICATORS FOR USE BY UNIVERSITY MANAGERS

	Users of Performance Indicators		
	Depart- ment	Cost Centre	Institution
Teaching and Research			
Cost per FTE student			
Research income			
Contribution to postgraduate and professional training	X	X	X
Submission rates for research degrees	X	X	
Number of research and sponsored students	X		
Occupation of graduates after 12 months	X		X
Undergraduate wastage rates	X		X
Occupation of graduates after 5 years	X		X
Analysis of publications/patents/ agreements/copyrights	X		
Citations	X		
Peer review	X		
Editorship of journals/officers of learned bodies	X		
Membership of research councils	X		X
Costs per graduate	X	X	X
FTE students to FT academic staff	X	X	X
Equipment costs per FT academic staff	X	X	X
Other			
Administrative costs per FTE student			X
Premises costs per PTF student			X
Library costs per FTE student			X
Careers services costs per FTE student			X
Medical services costs per FTE student			X
Sports facilities costs per FTE student			X
Other central costs per FTE student			X
Ratio of support staff to academics	X	X	X

Source: Committee of Vice—Chancellors and Principles.
          First statement by CVCP/UGC working group.

61

4   WHO SHOULD BE ACCOUNTABLE FOR WHAT AND TO WHOM?

As stated in Chapter 2, the desire to improve public sector accountability has under-pinned all the developments reviewed in that chapter. This pressure for increased accountability was not, however, stimulated by the desire to control legal or ethical behaviour as might have occurred following significant scandals or cases of fraud. The call for increased accountability was inspired by an economic rationality - the need to get better value per £ spent on public services at a time when it was perceived that there were likely to be less £s to spend. In this chapter the changing nature of accountability is examined in more depth. First, the various conceptual dimensions of public sector accountability will be explored, then the situation in both central government and local government will be examined in turn. More emphasis will be placed upon the relationships between central government and local government because that is where the main debate and issues currently focus.

A Conceptual Framework for Accountability

The fundamental notion of accountability is very straightforward. Some person or party is entrusted with some resources and that person or party has subsequently to give an account for its use (or non-use). There is implicit in this relationship, the existence of a superior authority who both grants the resources initially and has power to exercise sanctions for performance that is inadequate in some way. As the concept of accountability is explored, however, it can be seen that this general concept can be applied at various different levels.

Stewart (1984) provides a very clear analysis of the different levels at which accountability relationships occur. He argues that there is a ladder of accountabilities and, by implication, suggests that unless we break down our discussions about accountability from the usual generalities to consider what is required at each rung of the ladder, little practical progress will be made. Only by identifying clearly with which rung one is concerned, at any particular instant, can one begin to establish the relevant parties to that level of accountability and who should exercise sanction over whom. Stewart's ladder is shown in Figure 4.1.

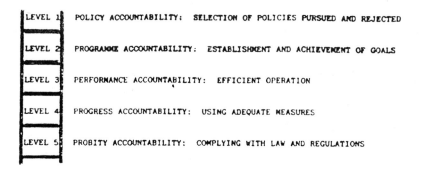

FIGURE 4.1   STEWART'S LADDER OF ACCOUNTABILITIES

The basis of Stewart's ladder of accountabilities is very straightforward. He identifies first that society agrees to the establishment of certain public sector activities to provide social needs. It is impossible to meet all needs and so choices must be made between competing claims. This gives rise to the selection and rejection of policies and the entity is accountable to society for the selection it makes.

With policies clearly established the responsible entity must establish programmes by which to pursue policies. This will lead to the establishment of goals, interpreted here to mean targets to be achieved by certain dates, and the means by which those goals will be achieved. This involves resource allocation between competing claims. This is not the same as the competition between policies, rather it is a competition between the need for resources necessary to pursue those policies.

Stewart's third level of accountability focuses more on efficiency of performance. That is, given the allocation of resources, does the entity produce the required outputs - is the input-output ratio good enough? Following that at level 4, one may enquire whether the procedures used to perform the operation were the best available, whereas level 5 is the traditional sense of accountability focusing upon the use of funds for the purposes intended irrespective of the efficiency with which those funds and resources were employed.

The hierarchical nature of the ladder is useful in depicting the different organisational levels of accountability, although one would probably reverse the ordering of levels 3 and 4. It seems that decisions about appropriate measures to employ would more usually be at a more senior level to more routine operating decisions. The ladder also clearly distinguishes between political accountability (more at the top end) and managerial accountability (more at the bottom), although care should be taken to avoid a simple dichotomy. Ratepayers, for example, will be interested in performance at all levels of the ladder. They may well exercise sanctions over major fraudulent practice, considerable inefficiency or inadequate measures or programmes. It would normally, however, require a materially significant fraud or inefficiency for the electorate to take such action; more routine monitoring of accountability at the lower levels of the ladder would usually be exercised within the service organisation.

This model of accountability then suggests that different people or interest groups and certainly different information sets are involved at different levels of accountability. Moreover, Stewart points out that there is a difference between what he calls a bond of accountability and a link of account. The latter involves only the right to information and the duty to report, whereas bonds of accountability carry with them the right to exercise sanctions. It is clear that there is scope for differences in both

64

bonds and links at different levels of the ladder. In fact, the ladder itself provides the basis of a framework for setting about the task of acquiring a comprehensive system of accountabilities and bears some similarity with the dual control loops of Figure 3.1.

Some would, no doubt, argue that the ladder reflects a strongly managerial way of looking at the world and that political reality is such that significant resource reallocations often arise from events relating to lower levels of the ladder and associated political pressure, especially where the need arising is urgent and unforeseen (eg responses to the Falklands, the riots of St Paul's, Bristol or a local epidemic or scandal). Nevertheless, such responses do imply some policy orientation even if not clearly formulated in advance and, at least after the event, the various accountabilities come into play. Moreover, while Stewart's ladder does seem to have similarities to the rationalisation structure of PPBS long left aside, he is not, as far as the author understands, advocating any particular sequence for construction of plans, he is merely identifying the different levels involved.

Stewart warns us against searching for universal solutions to accountability and proposes careful and separate assessment of each level. There is also a case to be made that, even at any specific level of accountability, what may be needed in terms of bonds of accountability, links of account and relevant information should vary from service to service and locality to locality. According to the type of public service offered there may well be differences in both interest and competence of taxpayers to assess performance. Equally the different technologies with, say, some associated aspects of defence may be so different from, say, social welfare services that different management structures are needed, quite apart from differences in secrecy and security. It follows that there may be the need for different emphases in systems of accountabilities for different services.

Similarly, the emphasis on accountability deemed appropriate to a County Council like, say, Wiltshire, may well be different from that required by the stakeholders of Liverpool. This notion of 'situational' systems of accountability has not (to my knowledge) been researched rigorously and so little more on the topic can be said here, but it should not be assumed from Stewart's ladder that standard systems of accountability can be imposed across all services and locations. Once again, Stewart indicates a general model indicating the various levels involved. The application of the model and the degree of similarity or difference in terms of locational requirements depends on a comparison of detailed empirical study of factors relevant in different contexts. Notwithstanding these warnings, the Stewart framework still facilitates some broad description of accountability in both central and local government.

Accountability and Central Government Expenditure

In terms of Figure 4.1, the main variable elements of accountability over central government activities has traditionally focused upon levels 1 and 5. Policy accountability operates through the electoral system. Within the system of Government, Ministers personally hold power over and legal responsibility for the acts of their ministries even though they meet collectively in Cabinet. Ministers are then accountable to the elected assembly of Parliament - to members of all parties including their own. The nature of the process has traditionally been, however, that politicians are more interested in raising colourful issues of direct political, and hence electoral, consequence. Moreover, the traditional incremental form of resource allocation made it difficult to deal with accountability of programmes through such a forum.

The fifth level of accountability, probity and legality, is also

66

strongly entrenched. This followed major reform introduced by Gladstone in the 19th Century. Parliament approved appropriations, the Treasury exercised control, the Comptroller and Auditor-General conducted regularity and compliance audits and provided reports to the Public Accounts Committee which had power to call for documents, interview senior Civil Servants, etc and make recommendations back to Parliament. Hence his 'circle of accountability' was established. The system was, despite some claims by the Exchequer and Audit Department to have conducted broader efficiency and effectiveness audits for years, essentially designed to check on probity and compliance with appropriations. There was relatively little concern until recent years with the efficiency of operations within each appropriation head. Also the ground which could be covered by the PAC was limited and so, even where it considered questions of possible waste and inefficiency, there was no comprehensive system of efficiency and effectiveness control for central government departments. (A more detailed description is provided in Pugh, 1986.)

In the 1960s and 1970s, therefore, it was realised that there was a marked absence of any systematic approach to accountability for Stewart's levels 2 to 4 across all government activity. Various attempts were made (The Fulton Report 1968, the PES system and the Heath era with the Central Policy Review Staff (CPRS) and the Programme Analysis and Review (PAR) system) to stimulate change, but the potential value of these mechanisms as systems of accountability was never realised. It was not until the 1980s that the pressure on public expenditure from two major increases in the oil price and the two Thatcher administrations began to make inroads into forms of accountability designed to tackle questions of managerial efficiency and, to some extent, programme and effectiveness accountabilities.

The new 1979 Thatcher administration, therefore, set about the task of, mainly, tackling levels 3 and 4 of Stewart's ladder. As described in Chapter 2, the Rayner scrutinies and the FMI were aimed at removing waste and inefficiency. Mrs Thatcher did not follow the Heath PAR route or the earlier grand designs of PPBS. Where she could not privatise, she placed prime reliance upon private sector management accounting logic. In particular the FMI was aimed to be a comprehensive system of managerial accountability based on principles of private sector responsibility accounting. Only now is it being extended into a more comprehensive system linked to longer term planning and this, if successful, will start to improve accountability at Stewart's level 2. It should be said, however, that these developments are very much a system of internal, managerial accountability. It is very difficult for those outside the Civil Service system, and especially the general public, to ascertain exactly who is accountable to whom for what. It is, of course, still an early stage in the development of the FMI. Possibly as it gets established and if it proves its 'worth', it will, coupled with advances in information technology, lead to a much more open system of accountability, public reporting and freedom of information across all levels of accountability. Indeed, looking 15 to 20 years ahead, one might risk a prediction that such a structure of more open accountability will exist. Meanwhile, there is plenty of scope for development work to explore alternative management structures and information and communication systems for achieving it.

There has also been a change in emphasis and formal status of the National Audit Office - indeed it was not called the National Audit Office, but the Exchequer and Audit Department, until 1983. As mentioned in a footnote in Chapter 2, the Conservative Government really did not see this development as a key plank in its policy of improving accountability. The National Audit Act of 1983 came about as the result of a private member's bill at a time when a general election was impending and so the Government was prepared to accept a number of its provisions quickly without major opposition - in return for the deletion of more controversial aspects. The general effect of the 1983 Act was to make the NAO more independent of the Government Executive and to confirm the broadening scope of national audit beyond regularity (level 5) into questions of efficiency (levels 3 and 4) and effectiveness (level 2). Section 6(1) of the 1983 Act says:

"The C&AG may carry out examinations into the economy, efficiency and effectiveness with which any department . . . uses its resources."

This was, however, really just a confirmation of existing and developing practice. Normanton (1966) had described the advances of initial audit beyond question of regularity. Indeed the C&AG's right to undertake broader reviews was questioned in the 1930s and each time the Public Accounts Committee supported the C&AG and the Treasury agreed. Nevertheless, the matter has now been put beyond all doubt.

The practice by which the Exchequer and Audit Department pursued questions of efficiency and effectiveness is, however, worth a comment. It did not take a top down view from overall policy questions. Rather it traditionally allowed questions of efficiency and effectiveness to 'grow out of' issues identified during regularity reviews. Moreover, it strongly asserted that it did not have the role of questioning policy, although, of course, issues raised relating to efficiency and effectiveness could easily lead to a reconsideration of policy by senior Civil Servants, Ministers and politicians. Such a process usually meant, however, that the focus was an accountability at levels 3 and 4 rather than 2. More recently, however, more NAO resources have been focused upon value-for-money reviews of key areas of activity. These have involved special teams of auditors engaged for longer periods on centrally selected issues deemed to be of key importance. Also the objective is now to show the degree of assurance which Parliament can place on the conduct of such activities and not just to report faults and activities. (Much more detail on these developments is provided in Keemer, 1985.)

Clearly, with annual expenditure subject to audit of over £100 billion, the NAO's approach to audit at levels 3 and 4 has to be highly selective. Nevertheless, the results of that aspect of accountability are more visible through the reports to the PAC than is the increasing managerial accountability through the FMI.

As an overview of the solution in Central Government, significant steps are being taken to improve managerial accountability at levels 3 and 4 of Stewart's ladder but, with such a range of activities as those controlled by Central Government, it takes time to set up the required modifications in both activities, information systems and control mechanisms. While there is still much to be done at levels 3 and 4, the least developed area in terms of general public accountability seems to be level 2. It is anticipated that this will also gradually improve from developments of the FMI as budgets and functional plans are now incorporating 'forward looks' over the period relevant to the current Public Expenditure Survey dates and beyond where appropriate.

Accountability and Local Government

The topic of accountability of local government has been much more newsworthy over the last few years than that of central government. This has largely arisen through the efforts of the Central Government to control local authority spending within limits which were consistent with its economic policy. Local authorities, not so directly concerned with national macro-economic policy, perceive the need for freedom to act to solve local problems and meet local needs. The increased intensity to contain public expenditure since 1979 has brought this natural tension between local and central needs and goals into sharp relief and led to the escalating series of Central Government interactions (cutting grants, rate-capping, etc) as described in Chapter 2. Also, as explained in that chapter, the Conservative Party often states that it is interested in giving more autonomy to local authorities if it could ensure better local accountability to act as a natural break upon inefficiency and excessive spending. The key question is whether such an effective system of local accountability can be found. Before addressing the question directly, it will be useful to contrast the basic structure of accountability in local government with that of central government. (Readers requiring more than the summary offered here are referred to the Widdicombe Report, The Conduct of Local Authority Business.)

As explained in the previous section of this chapter, Central Government is organised around a Ministerial system of accountability - power is legally held by individual politicians. This is a stark contrast to the position in local government where decisions are taken corporately on behalf of the whole council. Executive decisions are, therefore, taken by the Council whereas Parliament does not take executive decisions. Centrally, Ministers are accountable to Parliament, but do not act on behalf of Parliament in the way that local authority chairmen of main committees act for the Council. Consequently, at local level, the Council is supreme; it delegates power to committees or individual officers, but can override them. Interestingly, the Council has no power to delegate functions to individual councillors. In so far as the latter, especially as Committee Chairmen, take decisions 'between meetings' they must be able to carry these committees, and subsequently Council with them.

This way of organising the general structure of local accountability has been criticised by many. The Widdicombe

Report groups these criticisms under three headings. First, there is the accusation that the processes of decision-making in the Council become a 'hollow ritual devoid of substance' where there is a large political majority by one party which effectively takes decisions 'behind closed doors' and merely ratifies them in Council giving the appearance of general consensus and providing no viable or audible debate of the options and issues. It also seems to be wasteful in time to go through such a charade. Moreover, it places officers, as servants of Council, as effectively the servants of the political majority.

The second set of criticisms focus more directly upon the process of bringing people to account for their actions. If the Council is the executive body, it cannot be accountable to itself. Where there is a clear separation of the executives (eg Ministers in Central Government) from the elected assembly, there is a continuous scrutiny of action. If there is no such separation, it is agreed that accountability can only be exercised periodically at election time. Of course, political minorities will raise issues and attempt to create public consciousness over issues of concern, but legally even they are part of the Council which possesses executive authority.

The third heading of concern raised by the Widdicombe Report relates to the lack of efficiency in the process of local government administration. By international standards local authorities over Great Britain average 48 Councillors per Council (75 - 100 in larger authorities). As the Council is the executive as a corporate body, this makes it difficult to pinpoint accountability to individual people and also, it is claimed, leads to an unwieldy management process. Even the UK Cabinet has only 22 members and, the Widdicombe Report says, boards of major companies normally have fewer than 20 members. Local government abroad also favours small boards or even executive power resting in a city mayor or manager. The 'chief executives' of local authorities are, therefore, misnomers. They are, legally, chief coordinators of the Council's officers and not head of the executive which is, effectively, the leader of the majority party. The 'chief executive' role is to see that officers are sensitive to and carry out the Council's policy.

The Widdicombe Report examined the alternative to such a system and concluded that the existing system should be retained. With regard to the Ministerial system, it was stated that, in principle, it would be possible to create executive 'Ministers' for each main service from amongst the elected members who would then be accountable to the Council. Moreover, it would provide for special decision-making and sharper accountability. There would be no need to process everything through committees and these 'ministers' could form collective 'cabinets' to formulate general policy. Indeed, the Report says, this is effectively what already happens in some authorities without the legal formality being attracted to it. On the other hand, much of the current open-ness of information and facility for wider political participation in decision-making through the Council would be lost. Indeed, it was stated earlier in discussing Central Government accountability, that public knowledge and awareness of accountability processes and content at levels 2 to 4 is quite limited.

The Widdicombe Report also compares the current systems in local government with that proposed by the Maud Committee in 1967. That Committee recommended the appointment of a Management Board of 5 to 9 leading councillors as the executive. Once again it was claimed that this reflected reality, provided sharper accountability for those who really made the decisions and increased the efficiency of the decision process by removing a lot of the routine decision-makers from Council. Following much opposition from local authorities themselves, the Government did not accept the Maud proposal, but the Local

Government Act 1972 and the Local Government (Scotland) Act 1973 did give local authorities power to determine their own internal organisation and, with some exceptions, delegate such functions to committees and officers as they wished.

Finally, the Widdicombe Report examined a third alternative to the existing system called 'separation of power'. Under such a system, common in the USA and West Germany, the local authority executive is either elected or appointed separately from the general elected assembly. These executives then act within a broad budget framework and general policy established by the Council with full accountability to it. This could be introduced by making the current 'chief executives', chief executives in law and fact, but this seemed too much of an infringement upon current democracy for the Widdicombe Committee to consider.

As already stated, the Widdicombe Report recommended the retention of the Council as the corporate executive with decisions taken openly in Council and Officers as servants to Council and not individual committee chairmen. Apparently the great majority submitting evidence to the Committee were against any change. The Widdicombe Report itself stresses the flexibility of the current system. A Council can now, in fact, operate as Maud proposes or in a way closely according to the Ministerial model if it wishes. There is, however, the power of Council to restore the full corporate executive power if it deems it necessary. Management consultants, in fact, have considerable freedom in advising Councils how to structure their management processes and use their power of delegation and this can reflect local circumstances. Over-prescription by legislation of the structure by which executive power is actually exercised would prevent this. Current degrees of accountability in local government are, therefore, much more to do with informal processes and local interpretations of the power to delegate than with formal legalistic structure. Indeed there is plenty of scope for research

74

or consultancy to compare the process and methods used in different authorities and their effects on accountability. This would help to solve the question raised earlier as to whether this can be a viable general theory of accountability structures, a theory based on a few contingent factors or whether the appropriate forms must be highly situational.

Of more concern to the current Government in terms of local authority accountability is to consider what is needed to constrain expenditure levels to be sure that value-for-money is indeed achieved and waste removed. There seems to be no *a priori* reason why any of the forms of executive operation described above should necessarily be superior to the other in this regard. All forms of executive within the organisation of a local authority may exhibit forms of slackness unless there is some external pressure to perform well. One needs, therefore, to consider the effectiveness of the local 'election' system and arrangements for financing expenditure in terms of providing this external pressure.

The Government has recently issued a Green Paper 'Paying for Local Government' which proposes a fundamental change in the local taxation system. The Green Paper emphasises that of 35 million electors in England only 18 million pay rates and of those only 12 million pay rates free of any rebates or assistance. Moreover, of the £30 billion spent by local government each year, 40% came from Central Government grants, 30% from charges for services and housing rents and only 30% came from ratepayers. Even within the 30% paid by ratepayers, domestic ratepayers who have the vote only contribute about 12% of the funds for total local government expenditure (Hale, 1986). The balance of rate income comes from companies and other non-domestic ratepayers which do not have the vote. Consequently, it is argued that, local electors bear relatively little of incremental expenditure incurred by the authority or benefit much from cost savings. It

75

is not surprising, therefore, that there is little electoral pressure locally to constrain expenditure as reflected by the low turnout in British local elections, which fluctuates between 35 - 50% of eligible voters. This is much lower than the 76% of UK general elections or European local election turnouts. (But, it might be noted the turnout of local electors in the USA is, on average, only 35%.) As a consequence, it seems that Central Government feels that currently it is the only effective outside pressure on the achievement of cost containment.

Care must be taken with this argument. What is critical in terms of the burdens perceived by local ratepayers is not the proportion of local expenditure financed out of rates, but the proportion that rates are of their disposable income. There is considerable variation in the absolute amount of rates raised in different areas as well as marked variations in income levels. While clearly a change in balance of local authority financing to place more emphasis on the form of tax raised locally would increase consciousness of local spending, the impact of such a move itself, would depend on its effect on the percentage of disposable income paid away as rates.

As was made clear with the publication of the Green Paper, the Government is not in favour of replacing rates by a local income tax. It has, however, indicated that it wishes to introduce legislation at an early date to replace the rates system by a flat rate community charge on each elector in the locality coupled with (i) a nationally set non-domestic rate which would be pooled and redistributed to local authorities on a per capita basis and (ii) a revised government grant system whereby no government contributions will be made towards spending above specified 'needs levels' such that, with the fixed non-domestic rate, the entire burden of marginal increases will be borne by domestic community charge payers. This proposal has met widespread opposition from the Labour Party, CIPFA and various other associations.

The key question is, will such a revision increase local voters' interest and concern with local authority spending. Will it provide the clear link needed between increased local spending and the local responsibility for that spending?

First, there is likely to be a wide range of differing effects across local authorities. If a local authority finances a very low percentage of its spending from contributions from local voters, a marginal excess of spending over the 'needs level' will have a much larger impact upon the voters' burden. Hence, the effect of the scheme may be quite variable across the country; the degree of voters' interest and concern gained will be variable, as will be the scheme's ability to get all authorities' adherence to macro-economic spending policy.

Next, Ward and Williams (1986) argue that the Government's proposal to use a general inflation index to control increases in the non-domestic pooled rate income will result in a gradual shift of burden from non-domestic to domestic taxpayers without any increase in spending as local authority spending, being labour intensive, tends to increase more rapidly than the general index. Hence, this acts against the objective of a clear link between changes in local spending and changes in local taxes on voters.

It is also clear that the proposed new system would increase local direct taxpayers by about 100%. While this is so and might, therefore, stimulate wider interest in local authority affairs, one has to bear in mind that the incidence of the current rating system is not restricted to those who happen to pay the tax directly to the local authority - a large part of rates will be passed on to those in rented accommodation. In addition, the Widdicombe Report conducted a survey of public attitudes towards rates and, to quote:

"Most electors who do not themselves pay rates are members of a household that does. Second, many electors perceive of themselves . . . as 'ratepayers'."

Moreover, current direct payers of rates should find their contributions decreased on the introduction of the scheme if more persons are to be taxed. It has, therefore, been questioned whether the new system will not actually dilute the existing level of interest, rather than raise it. If the net effect is a significant drop in taxes paid locally as a percentage of disposable income, this may be so. This argument tends, however, to confuse absolute effects with marginal effects. The Government, it seems, is not seeking substantial reductions in expenditure from current levels (at least not at the moment); it is seeking to make <u>increases</u> in expenditure more subject to public pressure and scrutiny. While the new system may initially reduce the contribution of existing ratepayers, once the system is established, the amount each voter pays will change more significantly as a local authority decides to increase or decrease spending.

Finally, one needs to note that the Green Paper is retaining the option of capping community charge levels and so, it seems, it is not confident that all authorities can be constrained effectively by the new system.

At the time of writing (late November 1986), the Government has recently made its intentions more clear. It has already announced The Abolition of Domestic Rates (Scotland) Bill which will apply the principles described above. Also, the Government proposes that legislation be extended to England and Wales in the next Queen's speech, whether it comes before or after the next general election, although the actual implementation timetable would have to be such that a new Government of different political persuasion would have time to reverse the decision.

Whether the system eventually gets applied and tested across the whole UK, therefore, depends on the result of the next general election. If the Conservative Government feels uneasy about this, it is to a large extent its own fault as Mrs Thatcher made rates reform an election issue as long ago as 1979 and yet did nothing about it. The new system if introduced will make a lot more people directly aware of local spending through the very act of paying local tax, but the author's own view is that the strong local accountability which the Government purports to seek will not be obtained until local taxation is a somewhat larger proportion of personal disposable income. If the Central Government feels that it can effectively control the level of Central Government expenditure it has little need for taxpayer pressure to comply with macro-economic spending policy at that level. Consequently, it might consider changing the balance of national tax to reduce the element paid by individuals and increase the amount paid by corporations. In compensation to corporations it could relieve them of rates and place the extra burden on domestic voters - by way of a community charge, local income tax or other form of levy as desired by the political party in power. Hence, without increasing either the national or local tax levies in aggregate, voters would pay much more of their tax locally and less centrally. Increments in local spending would then create much more interest. The author has never seen this proposal elsewhere. Obviously, while logically neat regarding the aggregate tax position, the local impacts could be highly variable according to the proportion of non-domestic rating now, but adjustments might be made through the grant system for such local resource differences. It might well be decided that such an upheaval to both the national tax system and the local tax system is too much to ask for the sole achievement of strong local accountability. In which case one wonders whether any new system of local taxation will achieve strong accountability. The key requirement is an increase in the amount of personal disposable income which goes in local tax (of any kind). If that is not achieved and local accountability remains a key political issue, it is not inconceivable that a Central Government of either blue or red sympathy removes a large section of local authority spending (like Education) from local government activity. Only time will tell how all this develops, but it is a fascinating scene to watch.

While Widdicombe and the proposed rates reform raise key issues about accountability in local government, they focus at the top levels of Stewart's ladder. Moreover they do not provide for a comprehensive view of accountability even at that level. The Conservative Government places the emphasis of gaining local voters' consciousness of aggregate spending changes, but there are always trade-offs; new expenditure can always be funded by cutting existing ineffective expenditure. In considering increases in total expenditure, the new cost conscious voter will need to be assured that existing expenditure is effective. This brings us right back to Chapter 3 and its proposition that there is currently a lack of widespread effectiveness evaluations in local government - certainly of a form which can be understood by either voters or most councillors. Interestingly, this line of argument also brings one directly to the emphasis which is currently being placed on local government matters by the Labour Party - ie it is calling for more evaluation of the quality of service. One finds, therefore, that both the Conservative and Labour Party approaches complement each other. Indeed, one is unlikely to have much impact without the other. If voters take a greater interest in local government spending, they need improved ways of evaluating the value of the expenditure incurred. If more effort is devoted to assessing quality, it is likely to lead to considerable demands for increased expenditure to remedy inadequate areas, if the main burden of the increased expenditure is not met by local voters. Also, without adequate rates reform, this will only serve to exacerbate the existing tensions between central and local government. A comprehensive review involving both effectiveness evaluation and reporting (possibly using some procedures outlined in Chapter 3) and reforming the financing of local spending is urgently required. Indeed, given the Labour Party's new found desire to make the limitation of inflation its key economic goal, is it too much to hope that the Conservative and Labour Parties might actually recognise the complementarity of their respective positions on local government control and cease to oppose each other so markedly on this question? The answer, unfortunately, is almost certainly 'Yes'.

Moving to lower levels of Stewart's ladder, level 5 is adequately catered for by existing mechanisms of legislation and audit and has been for some years. Levels 3 and 4 have been subject to improvement by the Audit Commission developments - indeed the Commission is now moving its operations into effectiveness monitoring. It is not clear yet, however, that the pressures for improved efficiency have been, in most authorities more than ad hoc investigations. Apart from the changes in DLOs and contracting out, it would appear that there have been no major changes by way of introducing new responsibility accounting procedures as the FMI is doing in Central Government. Possibly, local authority accounts are already broken down over sufficient headings to provide a close approximation to allocating costs to the person responsible. There is clearly, however, the need for more work on output measures if efficiency is to be monitored on a responsibility centre basis.

As one moves down the Stewart ladder, it is clear that more of the practice of accountability must be conducted internally - both through the management process and auditing. There ought, however, to be scope for improved public access to relevant information at all levels. Already, electors in England and Wales have power to question auditors on the accounts and the

Widdicombe Report recommends extending this to Scotland, but it would be difficult to use that mechanism to challenge the use of inappropriate measures to carry out services (Stewart's level 4) or detailed aspects of operating efficiency. Widdicombe proposes also an improvement in the public accountability of auditors' reports. A more formal requirement of auditors to report on a cyclical basis over all services on each specific level of Stewart's ladder (including the review of effectiveness management suggested in Chapter 3) might also improve what is actually in the reports - it might provide a more systematic basis for an outsider to review the operations of the whole authority than do the current ad hoc reports.

In closing this discussion, a brief reference might also be made to the Local Government (Access to Information) Act, 1985. This Act covers all decision-making meetings and even includes sub-committees. Agendas, minutes and written reports have to be available for public inspection although many authorities could advertise this fact more widely than they do. There is some evidence, however, that some authorities are now delegating decision-making to closed 'working parties' in order to avoid the intent of the Act. Perhaps, therefore, despite Widdicombe, the existing system of power to delegate is too flexible. No doubt widespread abuse would lead to case law or further legislation to prevent such practices. A requirement of auditors to report fully to each relevant committee or sub-committee on the authority's management practices at each level of Stewart's ladder (say, at least once every four years) might, therefore, make a strong contribution towards increased public accountability at all relevant levels. As stated earlier, it would certainly be interesting from an academic's viewpoint to see what variation in systems of accountability at each level exist amongst different services and local authorities. There would also be plenty of scope for imagination in designing such audits. Just reports on efficiency and effectiveness would not be enough. It would also be necessary to describe and evaluate the processes through which responsibility is delegated and conducted. The Audit Commission started along this route with its audit of overall management arrangements. While innovative and ambitious, this is too general to be of much use except in the most ineptly managed authority. The same principles applied separately to different levels of Stewart's ladder for different services could lead to a significant advance in accountability. Perhaps some auditors might try it as a discretionary audit in order to test the value of such an audit process.

5   PLANNING AND CONTROL IN PUBLIC SECTOR ORGANISATIONS

At the beginning of Chapter 2, it was recognised that totally rationalistic planning and control systems like PPBS had failed. The attempt to develop a tightly integrated plan in a top-down way by deriving all the organisation's action plans by direct deduction from a ranked set of fundamental objectives related to the purposes of complete programmes had been shown to ignore the reality of political, organisational and human life.   If, however, the notion of an organisation makes any sense at all, it must be because it offers collections of individuals or interest groups the possibility for achievement superior to that attainable by separate actions.   There must, therefore, be a strong sense of joint action.   Coordinated control doesn't just happen, it must be planned.

Also in Chapter 2, the review of developments in public sector management in the UK since 1979 raised a number of issues needing further attention.   First, there was the need to consider how to deal with the conceptual definition of effectiveness and its practical operationalisation.   Second,   the concept of accountability seemed in need of further development and consideration.

These two issues were addressed in Chapters 3 and 4.   Other issues were identified, however, which related more to the managerial practice of planning and control.   The question was raised whether the Conservative Government placed a tight link between its declared objective of reducing total public sector expenditure and its new developments in financial management. Moreover, possible conflicts were identified between encouraging 'specific local' innovation (the Rayner scrutinies and the reduction of waiting lists were taken as examples) and the need to establish a coordinated budget of priorities.   On the other hand, Chapter 2 also referred to the political difficulties that can arise in trying to feed down plans to meet overall objectives and the problems that exist in trying to turn decisions into effective action. In other words the very same issues which gave rise to the debates of the 1970s about comprehensive and coordinated rational planning systems versus the impossibility of avoiding the adoption of an incremental view to public sector resource allocation still exist. There still seems to be a need for coordinated planning, action and control geared to organisational goals despite the demise of PPBS. This chapter, therefore, will explore the current state of planning and control as practised in the public sector and relate it to a few recent, but key developments in the literature. No managerial panaceas will be offered, but the state of the art seems to be such that a better understanding of the respective roles of coordinated planning systems in the context of political, organisational and human realities seems to be emerging, which renders the old dichotomy between rationalistic (PPBS type) planning and incremental development simplistic and obsolete.

Official Views of Planning and Control in the Public Sector

Despite the criticisms of PPBS as a top-down, over-rational planning system, many publications, managers and consultants still think in terms of its basic building blocks and form of deductive logic when asked to describe what planning and control is all about. The National Audit Office Report (1986) on 'The Financial Management Initiative' shows clearly how the FMI was based on the principles of the classical control paradigm which also underpinned the PPBS ideas. Ministries were expected to identify clear objectives for their programmes, establish well-defined responsibilities for carrying out the tasks and measuring performance against those objectives. Similarly the Audit Commission's recent (1986) handbook on 'Performance Review in Local Government', uses the same traditional control loop as exhibited in Figure 5.1. With such strong support for the traditional control paradigm of management, one certainly cannot dismiss it despite the earlier debates. There are, however, still some signs of tentativeness about the value of such a logical model. In fact, the Audit Commission Report (1986) itself states:

> "As a concept it is very simple. Unfortunately, implementation is not so easy. It depends on the acceptance for the need for the management of output, and the ability to control and plan inputs, both of which may have to be carried out in a highly charged political climate and with changing levels of resources."

Also the NAO Report (1986, p8) indicates that in implementing the FMI:

> "Central government departments draw attention to difficulties created by imprecise, broad, policy objectives; the multiple objectives of programmes; and the difficulty of distinguishing the effects of a programme from other factors."

Also the NAO Report (pp 7 and 8) state:

> "Departments had made substantially greater progress in developing arrangements for assessing outputs and performance in relation to the objectives set for their administrative costs, which are currently calculated to account for about 13% of central government expenditure, than for the programme expenditure which constitutes much of the remainder."

The Report also recognises that there is a substantial judgmental
element in performance appraisal and that:

"There is no way in which the application of sound
managerial principles to public businesses can be
expected to 'take the politics out of politics'".

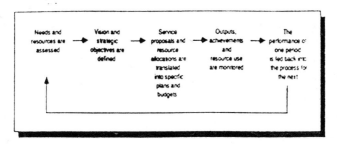

FIGURE 5.1   THE TRADITIONAL MANAGEMENT CONTROL PARADIGM
              (Source: Audit Commission: Performance Review
              in Local Government, 1986)

It seems, therefore, that those responsible for improving
management in the public sector recognise the arguments against
totally comprehensive rationalistic planning but, given that they
have responsibilities for achieving progress, still adopt the only
model of management that they feel has a general logic and
acceptability; despite its imperfections.   They do not have the
luxury of the academic who can sit back and point out the
defects of each approach, when not responsible for more cost-
effective management; they must work with the tools and
knowledge available.

A further argument for this adherence to the traditional model of
management is that in practical application it is not actually used

87

in such a rigid and stereotyped way as it appears when written or drawn as a diagram on paper. When this is recognised the stark contrast between rationalistic planning systems and views on the inevitability of incremental management begins to break down.

The model of control, such as that in Figure 5.1, is often seen by organisation behaviour experts (eg Morgan, 1986 and Kanter, 1983) as a direct descendant from Taylor's (1911) scientific management principles. According to these principles the concepts of controlling a machine are applied to the management of organisations: a task is set, the detailed systems and methodology is worked out, subordinates carry out the task in the way prescribed from above and output is measured against the task objective. This is often criticised as taking a dehumanising approach to organisational management such that subordinates have tasks heavily prescribed and are allowed little room for initiative. Hence, it is argued, the organisation loses capacity both to observe and adapt to the changing environment; often seeing the need to change too late. While organisation behaviour experts may be right to warn of the consequences of using such a rigid model of managerial control, this view of a 'machine bureaucracy' is but a caricature of the nature of most public sector service establishments. Granted some services are machine-like (this would include those that produce routine outputs which are easily measurable and a large part of the lower level administrative tasks, which interestingly the NAO found to be more advanced in terms of FMI development), but much of the public service provision involves professional judgment and local initiative where it is difficult to measure outputs in terms of relating them directly to broad level objectives of whole programmes. Such a situation is also a far cry from the thinking being performed at only the top of the organisation and those lower down merely doing what they are told as implied by the scientific management model. Consequently, the question arises as to whether the critics of rigid rationalistic planning are not in fact setting up a 'straw man'. The apparent, tight top-down logical structure of the simple control diagrams like Figure 5.1 disguise much of what actually happens when it is applied. This may mean that the control model of Figure 5.1 is not totally redundant; it just needs more sophisticated interpretation.

It should also be stated, in passing, that Figures 3.1 and 4.1 are also closely related to Figure 5.1 and yet they were deemed adequate to make the points addressed in Chapters 3 and 4. Drawings of models of control have exposition purposes of their own and must never be seen as complete mappings of reality. If they get over their message effectively, they need not address the rest of complex reality. Hence, one is really making a distinction between the description of the main building blocks to a rational planning approach as outlined by a model like Figure 5.1 and the attempt to apply it as the only means of practical planning and control through a comprehensive, rationalistic, top-down process like PPBS.

Good illustrations that practitioners are not so naive of political and other realities as their simple descriptions of management control would suggest, can be found in the recent publication 'good management in local government' produced jointly by the Audit Commission, the Local Government Training Board and INLOGOV (called below the LGTB Report for convenience). It has already been mentioned that when the Audit Commission was established it introduced a new audit related to reviewing the overall management arrangements of a local authority. This approach was based on the McKinsey model of good organisational management reproduced in Figure 5.2.

PLANNING AND CONTROL IN PUBLIC SECTOR ORGANISATIONS

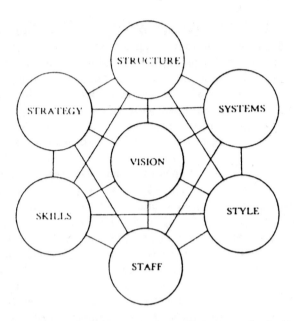

Economy, efficiency and effectiveness do not just happen. In almost every situation, changes – often uncomfortable changes, involving people doing things differently – will be involved. Those organisations in the public and private sectors which have been most successful in securing beneficial change have created an environment that thrives on challenge and change, by managing the following elements in such a way as to reinforce each other.

(i)   *Vision* what the authority is seeking to be or to achieve.

(ii) *Strategy* how this vision is to be translated into reality.

(iii) *Structure* the way the authority – its members, officers and staff – is organised to implement the strategy.

(iv) *Systems* the way in which the people in the organisation plan, decide, control and monitor day-to-day actions as well as longer term progress.

(v)   *Staffing and Skills* the way in which the critical resource in every authority – people – is acquired, trained, deployed, motivated and rewarded.

(vi) *Style* the 'way we do things' and the way members, officers and employees relate to each other and to those they are there to serve.

FIGURE 5.2   AN OVERALL VIEW OF ORGANISATION
              (Extract from Audit Commission Handbook)

Figure 5.2 illustrates that the organisation must have a clear
vision of where it is going based on the shared values of the
elements of the dominant coalition in the organisation and then
the strategies, plans and budgets, staffing, structures, systems
and management style must all be developed in a way which are
all simultaneously consistent with each other and with the
achievement of the vision. This diagram is an improvement upon
Figure 5.1 in so far as it moves beyond identifying just the
decision phases to indicate organisation variables like structures
and systems, but it still suggests a very close adherence to the
tightly coupled control paradigm where everything is geared to
objectives which now becomes 'vision'.

The LGTB and INLOGOV, not surprisingly in view of their
sponsorship by the Audit Commission, took Figure 5.2 as its
starting point and then elaborated upon how practices under each
element of the diagram can be reviewed by local authorities. It
is not appropriate to review here all the very useful advice
offered by the Report when those interested can read it for
themselves, but a few points will make it clear that the model is
not interpreted by the LGTB as though it were a model for
controlling a machine-type bureaucracy. In discussing vision, the
report addresses issues of inspiring leadership, committed staff
and the development of members and officers with public contact
so that they are aware of changing circumstances and effects of
action taken and feed them back into the management control
system. Under strategies, considerable attention is paid to
looking ahead so that there are not too many unexpected
surprises - hence strategic thinking is meant to overcome the
very defect attributed to the rigid adoption of 'scientific
management'. If the LGTB report sees strategy formulation in
this way, it is hardly recommending the adoption in Figure 5.2 as
the basis of operating in a rationalistic machine-like way. One

could give more examples, the Report draws attention to the need
to motivate staff and emphasise 'people and values' as much as
organisational routines while, under structures, it called for
delegation of responsibility to get officers 'close to the customer'
while retaining tight control over the level of performance in
general. Probably more than enough has been said to indicate
that the authors of the Report were quite aware of 'schools of
management advice' beyond the traditional 'scientific management'
model. In fact readers familiar with 'In Search of Excellence' by
Peters and Waterman (1982) will find phrases scattered
throughout the Report which are used to soften or modify an
unthinking, rigid approach to the implementation of the
framework in Figures 5.2 or 5.1.

It should be clear that the author feels that there is much high
quality practical advice which can be obtained from the LGTB
Report (1986). The same applies to The Audit Commission's
'Performance Review in Local Government'. Readers are urged to
examine both publications. Consequently, the commentary which
follows is not meant to belittle these Reports, but rather it is an
attempt to explore further the relationship between rational
planning and control and public sector realities. The LGTB
Report deals with this problem by recognising the realities and
trying to cope with them within the constraint of the traditional
control model. A relaxation of this contstrained perspective may
enable additional insights, although the end product of this
chapter will be to show that the basic building blocks of the
rational models should not be rejected, but subjected to
reinterpretation as to their role. To achieve this end, one needs
to consider the nature of resource allocation in public bodies in
more depth.

**Negotiated Order as a Missing Element from the McKinsey
Framework When Applied to Public Bodies**

It is now gradually becoming clear that the notion of
incrementalism was a necessary device for showing the
imperfections of a completely comprehensive, rationalistic
planning system, but it has offered little to act as an alternative
as a positive management approach. The concept of
incrementalism is of little value if it does not offer guidance on
how we should proceed to make spending decisions when
increments tend to be somewhat more than marginal with the
increased likelihood of squeezing out other expenditure options.
All increments of public expenditure are not marginal. Occasions
will arise when large changes in expenditure need to be
considered. In those situations, it will therefore be necessary to
employ some sort of choice mechanism which is capable of
evaluating competing options. Support of the incrementalist
standpoint seems to remove the rationalistic choice mechanism,
but does not provide an alternative one to put in its place. As
stated some time ago:

> "One is left with an unsatisfactory position: total
> rational planning is impossible, but incrementalism is
> only broadly descriptive and helps little in any quest
> to improve the resource allocation process".
>
> (Tomkins, 1980)

Also, as others have said, it offers no theory of the political
process underlying resource allocation - at very best it leaves it
implied (see Greenwood et al, 1977 and Sharpe, 1984).

Recent research referred to in Chapter 2 and conducted at the
School of Management in the University of Bath offers some

insights as to what the real world process of choice is in public sector organisations; although it must be stressed that the work briefly cited here relates only to decision processes in a few local authorities and Bath does not claim to be the only source of such knowledge.

First, Rosenberg and Tomkins (1983) provided a description of the processes which occur in the interactions between the Treasury representative, who has responsibility for liaising with the service department in budget determination, and the service department representative. Wildavsky (1975) had correctly captured the essence of the process with his argument that the Treasury had acted as guardian of the public purse and was there to challenge the need for expenditure, whereas the service department officer had the role of advocate for expenditure. But, at least at local authority level, the Rosenberg and Tomkins paper showed that that description only captured general tendencies within which occurred quite a complex series of interactions and negotiations. Indeed, there were occasions when the roles of the two officers seemed to be reversed as they tried to establish and reinforce a trust relationship to serve as the basis of a long run series of negotiations.

Next, Colville (1985) describes in depth the interactions which took place in a police force and police authority in considering resource allocation and the place of accounting in that process.

Following Weick (1979), he clearly shows first that the concept of 'an organisation' is itself far from an unambiguous concept. What the key persons in the police considered as 'we' differed according to issues considered. One gets the sense from the thesis that one is looking at an arena of events where different liaisons form to address different questions. Nevertheless, the situation is far from being totally fluid. Liaisons or groups do persist through time and groups that oppose each other or simply do not interact much at one level can come together to face environmental threats at another level. Also, this environment is not necessarily all powerful and determining; the environment consists to some extent of other groups which may or may not have common interests with our subject group. There is scope, therefore, for any group to attempt to influence the environment within which it operates and what is effectively the organisational boundary (in terms of 'us' versus 'them') varies according to the decision made. This throws increased light on why a total, organisation-wide, planning system can meet with difficulties, but also goes beyond that to show that decisions will be the product of different sorts of negotiations at different levels. Incrementalism indicates that changes from existing levels of resource allocation are determined by interaction between advocates and guardians, but it is only when one penetrates to the depth of empirical organisational analysis that, as Colville had done in looking at specific rounds of resource allocation, one sees the complexity of what actually occurs. Outcomes depend on the exercise of power in interaction with other individuals and groups although the exercise of immediate power is often leavened with the need to build longer run alliances and continuity of cooperation.

More recently, Williams R F (1986), in another Bath School of Management study of actual resource allocation procedures, also shows that the crude dichotomy between rationalistic decision-making and incrementalism is of little fundamental value in understanding what actually happens in public sector resource allocation. Williams reviews all the different strands of justification for the incremental view, ranging from the need to adopt an incremental perspective because human beings have limited cognitive capacities to arguments about the limited capacity to change ongoing activities and also political arguments which support the notion of incrementalism. His rigorous discussion concludes by dismissing them all as providing necessary conditions for the use of incremental approaches. Moreover, similarly to Colville, his empirical work shows how the fundamental resource allocation process is one of negotiated order. The main conclusion from Williams' work is that the degree of rationality or incrementalism which occurs in planning and resource allocation within a public sector organisation is very much a function of the desires of those with most power to exercise influence on decision procedures through the negotiation process.

The overwhelming view of this work at Bath is, therefore, that those involved in influencing the resource allocation process of a public sector organisation will perceive a given state of the world, but that there will be considerable scope for differences of perception to occur. More importantly, there will be different interpretations both of the significance of what is perceived and the extent to which the environment can itself be managed from within the organisation. This leads to a series of different goal orientations by those participants and the eventual allocation of resources can only be resolved through a process of negotiation. Moreover, the negotiation process is continuing and can result in variations in outcomes as the specifics of the situation change through time and location.

If models like Figure 5.1 and 5.2 are to have value, it is necessary, therefore, to relate them to the process of negotiation. Before considering this, it will be useful to consider one or two other developments in the management literature.

Why are some Organisations more Successful than Others?

Despite its central importance, the recognition of the point that negotiation plays in organisational decision-making tells us absolutely nothing about why some organisations are more successful than others. Moreover, successful achievement involves more than taking the right decision; it also involves successful action and implementation. When we turn to such questions there is reason to believe that it may be desirable to try to reduce the degree of negotiation which occurs in the organisation and, interestingly, the same set of arguments also seem to suggest some further relaxation of the tightly-coupled planning and control system suggested by a literal interpretation of Figures 5.1 and 5.2.

The book to have had most impact relating to re-thinking the secrets of organisational success is 'In Search of Excellence'. It has already been stated that there are signs throughout the LGTB Report (1986) of lessons learned from that book, but it will now be useful to give a more explicit consideration of Peters and Waterman (1982).

These authors commenced their study using the same McKinsey framework which serves as the basis of the LGTB Report (one of the authors was working for McKinsey & Co at that time). However, it must be stressed that this was only the starting point for their study, their research results lead them to the conclusion that organisational success depends much less upon totally coordinated, tightly-coupled planning systems and much more upon the way in which the general climate or culture of the organisation is handled. At the centre of their model of success would come the focus upon building the vision (or shared values or ideology) of the organisation, but they perceive it as

97

far more important that this is established and reinforced through informal contacts throughout the enterprise than it is to break this down through formal planning procedures into successively more refined strategies and targets.   Moving on from there, Peters and Waterman (1982) state that they observed eight key attributes possessed by successful companies:

1.   A bias for action: a concern to get on and put things right, rather too much procrastination.

2.   Keeping close to the customers' needs.

3.   Encouraging   autonomy   and   entrepreneurship   amongst employees.

4.   Recognising that productivity is mainly achieved through people and so there must be respect for the individual.

5.   Managers should use a hands-on/value-driven approach, ie make sure that they are seen around the organisation reinforcing the shared values by which they wish the organisation to be guided.

6.   Businesses should stick to the knitting, ie not take on other businesses which they do not know how to manage.

7.   There should be a simple organisational structure and a lean corporate staff function in comparison with the number of directly productive employees.

8.   Organisation control should exhibit simultaneous loose-tight properties, that is there should be a tight control over the core values to be instilled into all employees (eg an

overriding concern for product quality) but then as much delegation as possible should be allowed consistent with ideological requirements.

It is noticeable that the whole emphasis of these attributes is on the development of motivation and on building commitment of staff and employees to perform better within the broad set of shared values. This is seen as being achieved within a system which allows freedom of action and variety of decision, provided that that shared value set (eg organisation culture) is strictly observed. The focus is on action and experiment rather than too much tight control or analysis. While Peters and Waterman have not been without their critics, they did bring to popular attention a different emphasis in management. (A small district's efforts to move in this direction was described in Tomkins, 1985.)

A number of academics have written on this theme, both before and since Peters and Waterman, but there is one particular author who has recently published a development of the Peters and Waterman approach which serves as a relevant basis for further thought on this theme. Brunnson (1983 and 1985) like Peters and Waterman begins his book with a critique of rationalistic planning systems, but rather than just arguing for a de-emphasis of them, he is much more assertive in stating that they may often be quite dysfunctional to organisation success because they may reduce the effectiveness of the key factors needed for successful implementation of decisions. Brunnson also places an emphasis on obtaining successful ACTION AND ACHIEVEMENT; it is the end result which matters, that is the end effect of both decision taking and implementation, not just the former alone.

Brunnson's line of argument is that successful implementation of decisions depends on three factors: good motivation, high commitment to the action selected and common expectations of what is required and what should be achieved. He then develops a theory based on a number of case studies from both the public and private sectors which radically de-emphasises the degree of both rationality and negotiation needed in decision-making in successful enterprises.

Brunnson argues that when making decisions under conditions of uncertainty, extensive analysis of many options will only highlight the fact that much uncertainty exists and create greater uncertainty in the minds of organisation participants, thereby reducing commitment to action and motivation. Practising consultants will recall the phrase 'paralysis by analysis', but there is more to Brunnson's argument than that, for he continues to argue that decisions should much more frequently be based on an impressionistic basis, rather than on a comprehensive analysis of many options, provided that decisions made are clearly consistent with the general organisational ideology (ie visions or shared values).

An ideology is a straightforward concept in abstract terms, but it can have many different interpretations in practice. Brunnson argues for a very precisely specified ideology, which he calls a conclusive ideology. As an example, he describes (Brunnson 1983, pp 91 - 92) how one company set a very restrictive ideology such that only products and project proposals within a narrowly stipulated range were acceptable. The company ideology also recognised that marketing was its key to success in that particular set of markets and that sales were insensitive to price. There was a very clear conception of how customers made purchasing decisions and what the key desirable attributes of the products were. In fact, in Brunnson's own words, the ideology was a 'multi-dimensional model of the market' with 'elements which were strongly inter-connected in terms of cause and effect'. The written ideology also specified how these corporate goals were to be achieved, down to operational matters in some instances. It is very important to bear in mind what Brunnson considers a conclusive ideology to be for purposes of assessing the value of his argument a little later.

In addition to being conclusive, Brunnson argues that a strong ideology should be consistent, that is widely held throughout the organisation. It should also be complex, that is to say that, while it should be conclusive and definite, it should provide a full description of why that ideology is appropriate and perhaps even specify conditions in which the ideology would cease to be valid. A strong (ie conclusive, consistent and complex) ideology or vision therefore has a built-in mechanism to encourage its own self-adaption or destruction in due course.

Brunnson then argues that if an organisation has a strong ideology there is usually far less need to embark upon extensive rationalistic analyses where many options are sought and evaluated. Choices can be made on an impressionistic basis. Perhaps the term 'impressionistic' is unfortunate because Brunnson does not mean casual analysis. Impressionistic decision-making commences, with a decision-maker becoming aware of a few alternative actions or projects within the context of operating within his or her own organisation's ideology. On the basis of a few basic attributes of these possible projects, the decision-maker forms a strong view as to whether the projects are compatible with the current ideology and then restrains his or her information search to looking for data to support that initial view. When sufficient information has been established to support that initial view, the analysis stops. The approach is geared to moving to the action stage as soon as possible in order to reduce the need for extensive analysis, uncertainty creation and delay.

The process of impressionistic analysis itself also is directed to building a firm commitment to an action and reduce doubts. With a strong ideology it is both quicker and easier to make a more meaningful initial assessment and develop a supporting argument as the bounds of search and a detailed set of decision criteria are readily available making the obviousness of the 'right' decision emerge more quickly. It also implies through its less exhaustive enquiry that the organisation is prepared to make decision mistakes in terms of selecting optimal policies. Such marginal mistakes can be carried if enough broadly successful ones are completed. The more one focuses on taking action and getting things done in broadly the right direction, defined by the ideology, the more chance there is that this state of affairs will come about.

It is difficult from this abstract description of Brunnson's viewpoint to grasp exactly what degree of rational analysis he wants to abandon, but as this author was finalising this publication, an event occurred at home which illustrates exactly what Brunnson is trying to say. The example is trivial in comparison with decisions over social problems, but is still, it is believed, both graphic and germane in this discussion.

The author's family had decided to hire a house abroad for a summer holiday. Certain criteria were obvious; a house near a beach or with swimming pool, within specified price range, possible near some cultural interest, etc. A large range of brochures duly arrived and it was obvious within fifteen minutes that any one of 50 or more properties would provide the basis of a perfectly satisfactory holiday in accordance with the criteria set. There was no need for extensive rational analysis. To get an effective holiday, it was merely necessary to select two or three, check against basic criteria, check availability and act by booking. Things did not happen that way. Each member of the family embarked upon an extensive analysis and uncertainty escalated rapidly as to what action to take. Of course, fun was derived from the analysis and competing arguments. Probably a marginally better decision was eventually made and the author got 'brownie points' for being democratic, but, if one transferred that situation to all decision situations in a large organisation, where the joy of analysis should not be a measure of effectiveness, one begins to see precisely what Brunnson means. Clearly this author had not established a strong enough holiday ideology!

In summary Brunnson seems, like Peters and Waterman, to believe that successful organisations place rather more emphasis on setting out clearly their broad route and then focusing much more on getting things done to move along that route than on detailed analysis of alternatives. The key to getting things done is to create motivation, commitment and common expectations and it is primarily this that successful managers are good at. His theory also has strong overtones of consensus creation about it which suggests that some who argue that conflict within organisations can be profitable for the creativity it encourages, while not necessarily being wrong, may have to define very carefully where and when such conflict may be useful. It will probably arise much more in the creation and modification of an ideology, which by definition should be on an infrequent basis. Otherwise a state of continual conflict in debate or negotiation, may spill over into general personal relationships and prevent

103

consensus to action that Brunnson says so clearly is vital.

The matter of creating ideologies deserves a little more attention. Despite Brunnson's argument that strong ideologies build in their own modification mechanism, will not strong ideologies become so ingrained that they will be difficult to change? Brunnson says that this is not so because the more conclusive an ideology is the more it will be clear to everyone when it becomes obsolete in the light of changed environmental conditions. Also, the more consistent it is, the more likely it will be that a greater proportion of the organisation's people will see the ideology as obsolete and want change. Finally, the more complex it is, the greater clarity with regard to the conditions under which that ideology is appropriate. Strong ideologies, therefore, are not only more conducive to action within an ideological perspective, they are also more self adaptive.

An Evaluation of Action Rationality

Brunnson has certainly nailed down the lid on the coffin of totally comprehensive, rationalistic planning even more firmly than did Peters and Waterman. Bear in mind too that his theory is also empirically derived, grounded in observation of organisational practices. Nevertheless, in making his points in the way he does (and especially adopting the title of his book that he does) he runs the risk of considerably misleading practitioners into thinking that his theories suggest the rejection of nearly all rational analysis. Brunnson is against a rationalistic approach to planning and control with its implications of tight-coupling of actions, even at low levels in the organisation right through to global objectives and he is against too extensive a consideration and ranking of options. His alternative is a clear ideology and adoption of activities which clearly contribute in a significant way to that vision. Essentially he is saying 'get on and do something obviously useful and relevant, and don't spend too long thinking and analysing it'. Nevertheless, Brunnson does not make it clear enough just how much rational analysis[1] still lies behind his approach.

A strong ideology, in Brunnson's own words, is a multidimensional model with strong cause and effect links. Rational analysis must, therefore, be the foundation on which strategies stand. Next, even after ideologies are set, one must beware deemphasising the need for rational analysis too much. Some ideologies will themselves actually call for more rational analysis than others. Mrs Thatcher's ideological belief in the use of private sector accounting systems and forms of analysis obviously led to an increased emphasis on one form of rational analysis. Political opponents may argue about the desirability of the ideology, but once it was set and it was set very strongly as Brunnson would approve, officers had to comply in order to get their actions approved. Also one of the most fundamental ideological differences in our society at large over the last 200 years has been the tension between those pushing for greater efficiency and those emphasising the quality of life and 'culture'

---

1   The words 'rational analysis' are now being used to indicate simply the process of identifying cause and effect and should be distinguished from comprehensive planning systems which are said to be 'rationalistic' as defined earlier. This distinction is of <u>utmost</u> importance and the failure to make it has led to much confusion in planning and control debates. The rejection of rationalistic systems is not the same as throwing out all rationality.

in a more artistic sense (see Williams R, 1958). Moreover, one cannot deny that the efficiency ideology has brought immense advances from the industrial revolution to space travel. Putting a man on the moon required an action-orientated President of the United States to offer clear commitment before knowing how the task was to be done (hence supporting Brunnson's hypothesis), but the performance of the task involved an immense amount of rational analysis. Brunnson, therefore, does an excellent job of telling us to place more emphasis on action-rationality and less on decision-rationality, and at a broad level this is a valuable contribution, but his use of terms like 'impressionistic decision-making' and 'the irrational organisation' (as the title of the book) run the danger of disguising the fact that proposals for action must still be means-ends rational. He might have improved his argument by telling us to match the degree of rational analysis used to its criticality in making a satisfactory improvement in the achievement of objectives rather than stressing an 'impressionistic' approach. Finally, there seems to be no clear recognition of the degree to which negotiation lies at the centre of organisation behaviour.

Looking for Features of Real Life, Well-Managed Public Bodies

The selection of the heading for this part of the chapter may be misleading if it implies that the inner secret of managerial success is about to be revealed. This would be a foolish claim given our current state of knowledge. One can, however, try to make sense of the arguments developed in this chapter in order to see where comprehensive planning, negotiation and 'action-men' fit into organisation life. The matters raised in the remainder of this chapter are, therefore, offered as points for politicians, executives and consultants to ponder, rather than proven rules for success.

The current state of the literature on effective management may be summarised as follows. Until recently there was a direct conflict of view between, on the one hand, accountants, business planners and other 'rationalists' who wanted to develop tightly coordinated plans to ensure that organisational activity was goal-directed and, on the other, the more traditional 'behavioural views' which emphasised that staff motivation and freedom from detailed control was more critical to successful action. In this author's view, the main contribution of the more recent books of a 'behavioural nature' by Peters and Waterman, Kanter, Brunnson etc is to clarify how control and organisational direction can be combined with the requirements for successful action. This seems to be achieved by abandoning the pyramidal notion of control whereby all plans and activities are gradually broken down from the fundamental objectives of the organisation into successive layers of more detailed plans and activities all of which have to be authorised in detail by those in command of the layer above. This pyramidal notion of control is replaced by what one might call 'an hour-glass structure' of control. Organisational control is still seen in forms of hierarchical layers (although the fewer, the better) with the linkages between each layer in terms of detailed information and authorising procedures few in number. Those linkages that do exist are, however, tightly linked to the desires of the higher authority by focusing control on monitoring effectiveness achieved (ie results) and not on how it was achieved.

Applying this change in emphasis to a local authority, Figure 5.1 does not become completely redundant because it does remind us

107

of differences in level of decision-making, but it can probably be collapsed into just two stages in order to make the recent academic developments more visible. These two levels would be (1) The Strategic Level and (2) The Service Planning and Action Level. There must be a strong coordinating link between these two levels, but the links can be few (or narrow) if specified in terms of a strong ideology - hence the 'hour glass structure'.

(1)   The Strategic Level

This level would be a combination of objective setting, vision and strategy formulation. These divisions are artificial and unhelpful. Overall objectives of whole services are too vague and weak to be practically useful and as Brunnson says, one needs 'strong ideologies' (ie conclusive, widely-held and complex).

Strong ideologies are, however, no less than detailed strategies. Also, while members' and officers' basic beliefs will affect their vision, this process does not occur in a detailed way in isolation from the authority's current activities. Detailed strategies only make practical sense if they specify <u>precisely</u> changes from 'what we are doing now'. This would include situations where improved effectiveness is <u>not</u> required, but where threats exist and changes are needed to ensure maintained performance. It also does not mean that members have no view of the performance of ongoing activities; this would come from the effectiveness analysis, but strategies are about <u>moving</u> resources and preparing for <u>different</u> actions. It is interesting that logical planning in this sense facilitates not hinders the practice of incrementalism and gives it rigour.

Next, if ideologies are to be conclusive, widely-held and complex this may arise from a quickly emerging consensus, but more often there will be the need for considerable rational analysis and negotiation in formulating the ideology, otherwise it would not be a strategic issue. This is quite different from the call for less time spend analysing non-strategic decisions (the choice of a holiday house is not strategic, but the change of a permanent residence would be to most people). Council leaders and chief executives must see that ideologies are rigorously considered in order that they may be strong, which in turn enables them to be used to generate effective action.

Possibly the main role of a chief executive should be the facilitation of the development of 'strong' ideologies and advising leading politicians how to develop them in the local situation. This will also involve recognising situations where members feel that questions are merely matters of efficiency, but where others (ratepayers, clients and staff) consider the issue strategic. The effectiveness evaluations of Chapter 3 could play a significant part in this process.

Following Brunnson, one does not want to be 'too democratic' and have an excess of negotiation which wastes time and can raise uncertainty, but it is critical to recognise where negotiation is essential, who should be involved to ensure it is widely-held and how it should be conducted. Executives should give thought to the required processes by which 'strong' ideologies may be developed in their own authorities. The advice of the LGTB Report which effectively just says strategies should be negotiable only 'scratches the surface'. The LGTB publications on the 'Management of Hung Authorities' (1985 and 1986), 'The

Management of Influence' (1986) and Hinings (1983) all begin to address this problem, but it must be borne in mind that negotiation is not just needed where there is no clear political majority. There are other sources of power besides the voting mechanism, especially in the short-term. A careful assessment of the power of different interest groups is called for, prior to settling upon a set of ideologies/strategies.

Finally, the 'strong' ideology being expressed in terms of a precise change should provide its own basis for monitoring whether effective action has been achieved. Monitoring by results in this way enables the organisation to take advantage of the 'hour-glass structure' of control. The strategic level does not need to approve detailed plans and authorise detailed activities. Again effectiveness evaluations are crucial to this process and if ideologies are specified in this way in terms of precise changes from the current situation the evaluation process becomes easier, though rarely easy, to formulate.

(2)   Service Planning and Action Level

With 'strong' ideologies set and the Chief Officer's assurance that they are strongly held within his service department, one can dispense with a tightly-coupled system of control and authorisation over the service department's activities. Of course, even within a large service department the same 'hour-glass' principle could be used by the Chief Officer but, however many layers of delegation there are, control should be primarily by monitoring effects. At this level too, effectiveness will need to be evaluated on ongoing activities as well as specific strategic changes, but if ideologies are set strongly between layers, the planning process each year can simply focus upon changes in ideologies.

It is within the bottom half of the hour-glass that Figure 5.2 has more relevance. Here there will need to be a tight consistency between technical systems and steps needed to perform the tasks. If, however, the tasks are being designed at this level, these decisions are best taken at this level bearing in mind the resources available. In general it is hoped that Brunnson's view will hold and that significant improvements in attaining the ideology set will not depend on extensive rational analysis. The Chief Officer has a key role on educating his staff to recognise the concept of action-rationality, learning by experiment, and the dangers of over-analysis while at the same time being able to select situations where more analysis will yield significant benefits. The latter will probably involve situations where decisions affecting effectiveness to a considerable degree are not easily reversible or where more information on one key variable in the decision is vitally important. An action-orientation should, therefore, be one dominant aspect of style in Figure 5.2.

Formal structures probably need not be so tightly coupled with the ideology. What is important is the informal collaboration and attitudes of staff. It will, in the approach being described, probably be helpful to have task forces to address specific changes or improvements in satisfying ideologies rather than feeding everything through formal pyramidal structures. If this cannot be achieved informally, it may be necessary to change the formal structure.

Implications for Accountants, Managers and Consultants

First, it is clear that the traditional control paradigms expressed
in Figures 5.1 and 5.2 do have practical relevance. The attack
on rationalistic planning processes does not invalidate them.
They demonstrate where there is a need for consistency between
actions. They can be interpreted in various ways in terms of the
processes by which this is done and one reinterpretation has been
presented in the previous section of this chapter.

Next, practitioners of well managed organisations may feel that
this is obvious and that much of the material on the last section
is already practised. If so, that is fine; after all, these
principles were developed by Peters and Waterman, Brunnson and
others from observations of organisational practice. Also, if this
is widely practised, it is not adequately reflected in either
management or academic literature. Academics in the
management field and practitioners should feel uncomfortable
when statements like the following are published:

> "There are all manner of centres run by local
> authorities and other bodies which provide short
> courses for teachers in the public sector on
> 'management in colleges'. But the content of such
> occasions generally boils down to little more than
> saying that it is a good idea to know what you want
> to do before you start doing it."
>
> (Barker, 1986)

Barker may not realise how often this message does need to be
repeated, but the thrust of his criticism is appropriate. Figures
5.1 and 5.2 do not really say much more than this. To respond
to such criticisms more attention must be paid to the effects of

different <u>processes</u> which could underlie each decision and action
stage in different settings.

The previous sections of this chapter also have obvious relevance
for the issues raised in Chapter 2 relating to the need to
distinguish operational matters from strategic and manage the
taking of action as well as analysis. In so far as the
Conservative Government has insisted on much more extensive
accounting analysis, it may appear that runs counter to the
proposals of this chapter. This need not be so. The thrust of
the FMI is turning more and more to the achievement of results
and less to cost saving. Even so, cost saving is obviously
relevant, but it should be delegated as far down the hierarchy as
possible and managers at that level should be given the
accounting expertise needed to achieve that. This seems
generally what the FMI has attempted to do. The only caveat is
to devise routine ways of doing this so that the operating and
reporting systems themselves do not become so complex that they
detract from an action-orientation.

Also the 'hour-glass approach' will probably require a
reconsideration of budgeting procedures. If action autonomy is
to be encouraged, this must be coupled with budget autonomy.
Monetary resources must be allocated to service departments with
as little constraint as possible. This further seems to imply that
the budget setting process will become more competitive than it
often is now. If members and chief executives are not to get
into detailed reviews of service department activities and are to
manage more by monitoring effects, obligation will fall upon
service departments to bid for increases in funds and in so doing
make their case in terms of final effects specified as precisely as
possible. The control will be the follow up of effects.
Departments may then simply accept their lot and not bid for

improvements. The control over such behaviour would be the possible loss of funds to other active departments. The proposals would, of course, have to comply with the 'strong' ideologies set by the Council. This may seem like a return to detailed approval from above but it need not be if the focus is approval for resources for major changes. It also does not prevent the Treasurer's department checking on the continued relevance of the continuation budget, but this could be done less frequently, almost as an audit function, rather than using an integral part of the budget setting process with full line detail being considered by the Council. Such an approach has attributes of both programme budgets and incrementalism.

Finally, and this may be the most important message of all, the whole approach emphasises the need to return more of the process of managing to those who know the problems of service delivery and who have to act. While a general manager will be useful for his or her role in setting the 'strong' ideologies there should not be a plethora of managers who can do nothing but manage. Those with skills needed for service delivery must be taught to apply good management principles to their everyday tasks. The process of sharing out managerial responsibilities amongst service delivery staff will facilitate team building which in turn should stimulate initiative. This also implies that it is they who should have the prime call upon the assistance of the specialist functions like accounting and not them being called to account over details. Accountants (as distinct from the central treasury function) should have to demonstrate rather more to the service departments that their skills will lead to greater effectiveness.

The trouble with writing about management topics is that, despite one's intention to try to be tentative and suggestive, the lack of proven knowledge about the 'best way to manage' leads one to exhortation and it is easy to sound dogmatic. To the extent that this has been done in this chapter, it has resulted from trying to follow through the implications of some recent developments in thinking about organisations. There will always be unstated caveats and qualifications in a field such as this. This chapter merely hopes to persuade managers and accountants to think more about their practices and publicise their thoughts. In that way we may develop a better understanding of the processes which need to underlie almost naively simple diagrams like Figure 5.1.

REFERENCES

Bailey, E & Baumol, W J, Deregulation and the theory of contestable markets, <u>Yale Journal on Regulation</u>, 1984

Bailey, E, Price and Productivity change following deregulation: the US experience, <u>The Economic Journal</u>, March 1986

Barker, R, 'Rise of the great pretenders', <u>The Times Higher Education Supplement</u>, 4 April 1986

Brunnson, N, The irrationality of action and action rationality: decisions, ideologies and organisational action, <u>Journal of Management Studies</u>, 19, 1982 per HD.

Brunnson, N, The irrational organisation, Wiley, 1985 ILL

CIPFA, <u>A statement on performance indicators in the education service</u>, April 1986

Colville, I, <u>Men and their budgets: budgets and their men. An empirical investigation of accounting as interactions in a police authority</u>. PhD thesis, The School of Management, University of Bath, 1985

Domberger, S, Meadowcroft S A & Thompson, D J, Competitive tendering and efficiency: the case of refuse collection, <u>Fiscal Studies</u>, November 1986

Goddard, R A, <u>Company Acquisitions</u>, PhD thesis, The School of Management, University of Bath, 1986

Greenwood, R, Hinings, C R & Ranson, S, The politics of the budgetary process in English local government, <u>Political Studies</u>, 25, 1977

REFERENCES

Grimwood, M & Tomkins C, Value-for-money auditing - towards incorporating a naturalistic approach, Financial accountability and management, Winter 1986 AMB

Guba, E & Lincoln Y, Effective evaluation, Jossey-Bass, 1981
out
H 62 GUB

Hale, R, Local Government, in Public Domain, 1986, eds Mayston D and Terry F, Public Finance Foundation and Peat Marwick Mitchell & Co, 1986

Hinings, B, Planning, organising and managing change in local authorities, INLOGOV, 1983

Jarratt Report: Report of the Steering Committee for Efficiency Studies in Universities, CVCP, March 1985

Kanter, R M, The Change Masters, Simon and Schuster, 1983

Keemer, P, State Audit in Western Europe: a comparative study, MPhil thesis, The School of Management, University of Bath, 1985

Local Government Training Board, The Management of Hung Authorities, 1985 and 1986

Local Government Training Board, The Management of Influence-implications for management development, 1986

Local Government Training Board and INLOGOV, Good management in local government, Audit Commission, 1986

Madaus, G M, Scriven M & Stufflebeam D, Evaluation models, Kluwer-Nijhoff, 1983

H 62 MAD

REFERENCES

AMB

Mayston, D, Non-profit performance indicators in the public sector, <u>Financial Accountability and Management</u>, Summer 1985

Mayston, D & Terry F, (eds) <u>Public Domain</u>, 1986, Public Finance Foundation and Peat Marwick Mitchell & Co, 1986

Metcalfe, L & Richards, S, Raynerism and efficiency in Government, in <u>Issues in public sector accounting</u>, eds Hopwood A and Tomkins C, Philip Allan, 1984

Millward, R, The competitive performance of police and private ownership, in <u>The Mixed Economy</u>, ed by Lord Rolls, Macmillan, 1982

Millward, R & Parker, D, Public and private enterprise: comparative behaviour and relative efficiency, in Millward, R and others, <u>Public Sector Economics</u>, Longmans, 1983

Morgan, G, <u>Images and Organization</u>, Sage, 1986

National Audit Office, <u>The Financial Management Initiative</u>, HMSO, 1986   ILL

National Audit Office, Report of the Comptroller and Auditor General, <u>The Rayner Scrutinies, 1979 to 1983</u>, March 1986

Normanton, E, <u>The accountability and audit of Governments</u>, Manchester University Press, 1986

Oates, G, The FMI in central government, <u>Public Finance and Accountancy</u>, 20 June 1986

Peat Marwick Mitchell & Co, <u>Financial management in the public sector, a review 1979 - 1982</u>, 1984

Peat Marwick Mitchell & Co, <u>Current issues in public sector management</u>, 1986

Peters, T & Waterman, R, <u>In search of excellence</u>, Harper and Row, 1982

AMB

Pollitt, C, Beyond the management model: the case for broadening performance assessment in Government and the public service, <u>Financial Accountability and Management</u>, Autumn 1986

Pryke, R, <u>Public enterprise in practice</u>, McGibbon and Kee, 1971

Pryke, R, <u>The Nationalised Industries: policies and performance since 1968</u>, Martin Robertson, 1981

Pryke, R, The comparative performance of public and private enterprise, <u>Fiscal Studies</u>, July 1982

Pugh, C, <u>Reforms for efficiency in British Public Administration</u>, South Australian Institute of Technology, 1985 (privately circulated paper)

<u>Report of the Committee on the Management of Local Government</u>, 1967 (Maud Committee)

<u>Report of the Committee of Inquiry into the conduct of local authority business</u>, 1986 (Widdicombe Committee) CMND 1797

Rockhart, J, Chief Executives define their own data needs, <u>Harvard Business Review</u>, March 1979

Rosenberg, D & Tomkins, C, The budget liaison officer: guardian or advocate? <u>Local Government Studies</u>, September/October 1983

REFERENCES

Schmidt, R E, Evaluability assessment and cost analysis, in The costs of evaluation, eds Atkin, M and Solomon, L, Sage 1983

Scriven, M, New frontiers of evaluation, Evaluation practice, February 1986

Sharpe, L J, Incremental theory and budgeting: a model test, a paper presented to the University of Manchester seminar on Government Budgeting and stress, 1984

Singh, A, Takeover, natural selection and the theory of the firm, Economic Journal, September 1975

Stewart, J D, The role of information in public accountability, in Issues in public sector accounting, eds Hopwood, A and Tomkins, C, Philip Allan, 1984

Swarz, P A, Program devaluation: can the experience reform? in Measuring the hard-to-measure, ed Loveland, E, Jossey-Bass, 1980

Taylor, F W, Principles of Scientific Management, Harper and Row, 1911

The Audit Commission, Performance Review in Local Government, 1986

The Audit Commission, Economy, efficiency and effectiveness, regularly updated

Tomkins, C, Is there a role for effectiveness auditing in local government? (one of a series of CIPFA Centenary lectures, forthcoming)

REFERENCES

Tomkins, C, The effect of political and economic changes (1974-1982) on financial control processes in some UK local authorities, KMG Thomson McLintock, 1986

Tomkins, C, Value-for-money in the public sector: (1) Rationality vs incrementalism in budgeting, Local Finance, 1980

Tomkins, C, A view from the Mendips: a district council's vision of excellence, The Accountant's Magazine, August 1985

Tomlinson, J D, Ownership, Organisation and Efficiency, The Royal Bank of Scotland Review, No 149, March 1986

Van Gunsteren, H R, The quest for control, Wiley, 1976

Ward, L & Williams, P, Accountability: panacea or placebo? Public Finance and Accountancy, 17 October 1986

Wildavsky, A, Budgeting: a comparative theory of budgeting processes, Little Brown, 1975

Williams, R F, Incrementalism and the politics of resource allocation in local authorities, PhD thesis, The School of Management, University of Bath, 1986

Williams, Raymond, Culture and Society, Penguin, 1961

Wright, V, Public-privé espaces et gestions, a paper presented at the first Colloque International de la revue Politique et Management Public, December 1986 (available in English)